27in (68.6cm) Well-known Unknown, French bisque, ball-jointed body, paperweight eyes, human hair wig. This doll wears a sheer brown silk taffeta A-line dress with a finely shirred inset vest bordered with beige lace. The skirt features three ruffles of self-fabric, topped by a ribbon bow at center front. Completing the costume is a bonnet of buckram and wire covered with self-fabric and trimmed with fine beige lace over the shirred brim.

ABOVE LEFT: 14in (35.6cm) Jumeau (Réné reproduction), bisque, ball-jointed, stationary eyes, human hair wig, marked by Réné. This little doll is wearing a simple A-line dress which derives its charm from use of contrasting bands of trim from the sari as shown by the contrasting vest, collar, cummerbund and bustle (1886).

18in (45.7cm) Tête Jumeau (Italian reproduction), bisque, ball-jointed body, stationary eyes, human hair wig, marked by maker. This little doll is wearing a simple cotton plaid jumper and white silk guimpe with full sleeves gathered on a wrist band. The costume is topped by a jaunty "Scotch" cap (1887).

ANTIQUE
CHILDREN'S FASHIONS
1880-1900

A HANDBOOK FOR DOLL COSTUMERS

by Hazel Ulseth & Helen Shannon

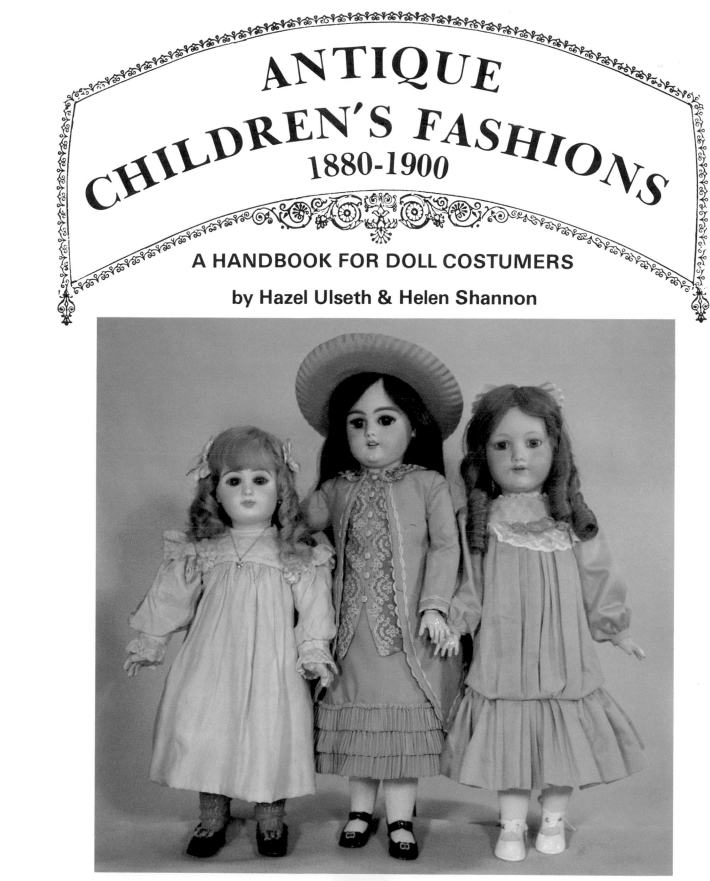

Hobby House Press

Published by

Cumberland, Maryland 21502

Dedication

To our mother, Ann Rebecca Johnston, whose later life was enhanced by our mutual interest in dolls.

SPECIAL THANKS to Lois Davis, a dear friend, enthusiastic doll collector and faithful supporter of our endeavors, for her many hours of typing and her meticulous proofreading.

. . . and to Robert Shannon for his endless services as postman-in-residence.

FRONT COVER:

RIGHT: 23in (58.4cm) Schmitt (?) French bisque, ball-jointed body, blue paperweight eyes, blonde mohair original wig, unmarked. Pale green silk long waisted dress with lace trim. CENTER: 20in (50.8cm) Steiner, French bisque, ball-jointed body, paperweight eyes, human hair wig, marked: STEINER//PARIS//Fre A 13. This Steiner wears a soft pink yoked silk dress with full skirt and little chatelaine of narrow ribbon dangling from the waist. LEFT: 22in (55.9cm) Schmitt, French bisque, ball-jointed body, paperweight eyes, human hair wig, marked:

Schmitt with a green silk satin dress featuring an insert at the neck with rows of featherstitching, and a period-styled chapeau (1880s).

TITLE PAGE:
LEFT: 19½in (49.6cm) ball-jointed body, paperweight eyes, human hair wig, marked: Tete Jumeau//DEPOSE//Tete Jumeau//Bte. SGDG 8. Original yoked pale pink silk dress with rosettes of silk ribbon. CENTER: 22in (55.9cm) SH 107 9 German bisque, ball-jointed body, sleep eyes, human hair wig, marked: SH 1079//10½-7//DEP. This doll is wearing an aqua blue silk polonaise over a full ruffle-trimmed walking skirt, with a "beefeater" hat. RIGHT: 24in (61.0cm) AM German bisque, ball-jointed body, stationary brown eyes, human hair wig, marked: Germany//A 390 M. Long waisted frock of lilac cotton sateen, long gathered sleeves, and lace-trimmed yoke.

BACK COVER:
LEFT: 18in (45.7cm) Portrait Jumeau, French bisque, ball-jointed body, paperweight eyes, human hair wig, marked 8. Sheer silk blue and white checked pompadour-style dress with short sleeves over a sheer silk guimpe (1888). CENTER: 27in (68.6cm) French Fashion (DeNunez reproduction), mohair wig, stationary blue eyes, kid body, marked by DeNunez. French Fashion: adult fashion of the 1880s in two-tone pink with beige lace, bustled top over full walking skirt. RIGHT: 18in (45.7cm) RD, French bisque, ball-jointed body, paperweight eyes, human hair wig, marked RoD. RD wearing a turquoise silk pompadour dress with contrasting velvet trim (1888).

LEFT: 18in (45.7cm) K*R Pouty (Réné reproduction) bisque, ball-jointed body, stationary eyes, human hair wig, marked by Réné. Pouty wearing an A-line moss green silk dress with elaborate bustle and cummerbund. CENTER: 17in (43.2cm) German or French bisque, ball-jointed body, paperweight eyes, human hair wig, marked DEP. German bisque wearing a two-tone rose silk dress, long waisted with yoke and diagonal trim (1888). RIGHT: 19in (48.3cm) K*R 117 Pouty (Réné reproduction) bisque, ball-jointed body, stationary eyes, human hair wig, marked by Réné. Pouty wearing a chocolate brown polyester pompadour with contrasting velvet trim over a beige silk guimpe, and a mob-type bonnet (1887).

ISBN: 0-87588-192-0

Table Of Contents

16in (40.6cm) RD, French bisque, ball-jointed body, paper-weight eyes, mohair wig, marked R 2/0 D. This lovely RD is wearing an A-line dress showing skillful use of an old deep maroon scarf with bands of woven multicolored trim and a lovely selvage. The inset vest was made of narrow bands of selvage, the cummerbund and bustle of the woven bands. Lace trim completes collar and sleeves, while the mob-type bonnet of maroon silk complements the maroon of the dress.

TOP LEFT: 14in (35.6cm) Reproduction Columbus 1981 Regional Souvenir A.T. ball-jointed body, stationary eyes, by Muriel Kramer. This frock from *The Delineator* 1899, designated Toddlekins, has a full skirt and features an unusual treatment of the yoke with a shirred and trimmed insertion bordered by charming bretelles. A shirred and wired bonnet completes the costume.

20in (50.8cm) Steiner reproduction, ball-jointed body, stationary eyes, human hair wig, and marked Neva Wade Garnett, 1980. This pattern features a high-waisted dress with full skirt and bouffant sleeves on long cuffs. An elaborately trimmed bodice features lace and ribbon trim radiating from a mandarin collar, lace-trimmed bretelles over the shoulders, and specially designed self-fabric bows.

14in (35.6cm) Kley & Hahn Walkure, German bisque, ball-jointed body, sleep eyes, human hair wig, marked: KH//Walkure//Germany. In an A-line dress of blue silk with lace-trimmed inset vest over a pleated skirt with lace and tab trim.

16in (40.6cm) K★R 101 Pouty (DeNunez reproduction), bisque, ball-jointed body, intaglio eyes, human hair wig, marked by DeNunez. Pouty with a turquoise silk A-line dress, lace-trimmed with lace ruffled over a silk pleated skirt.

24in (61.0cm) A.T. (Kramer reproduction), bisque, ball-jointed body, stationary eyes, human hair wig, marked by Kramer. A.T. showing a side view of a polonaise worn over a full walking skirt and a "beefeater" hat (1885).

List Of Illustrations

About The Authors

Hazel Ulseth, one of the authors of this book, has been dressing dolls for 25 years and has won many blue ribbons in costuming. She and her sister, Helen Shannon, have been working together for 15 years on doll costuming and share with pleasure some of their experiences in pattern-making and development of sewing techniques to make some of the tedious handwork a little more pleasurable.

ALL DOLL PHOTOGRAPHY WAS DONE BY HAZEL AND MARTY ULSETH.

Hazel Ulseth and Helen Shannon, sisters, are shown presenting their program-workshop, "Fashion Patterns" at the 1982 UFDC Kansas City doll convention.

Introduction

In the following pages of this handbook we endeavor to present a few ideas, illustrations and descriptions which will assist the "home" doll costumers in achieving a finished product with some degree of conformity and authenticity to period costumes contemporary with the manufacture of French bebes and German bisques.

In addition, we believe that many experienced doll costumers will enjoy some new and different approaches to trim, handling of lace and ribbon, styling, fit and some of our "Helpful Handy Home Sewing Hints" . . . leading to unusual treatment of laces and ribbons, self-fabric ruffles and fluting without a fluter.

We emphasize one point throughout our handbook. All doll collectors are aware of the ideal situation in which one has a beautiful antique doll in its perfect original garments. However, we recognize this as a rare situation. For those who cannot achieve this goal we hope, instead, to provide some satisfaction to doll owners by helping them to enjoy dolls enhanced by authentic fabrics and charmingly styled costumes. By all means, keep the old for reference, but enjoy the new.

So here you will find pages of pictures, patterns, descriptions of sewing techniques, ways of handling laces and trim which may be new to you, little hints and successful tricks to make the sewing procedure a little simpler, and less tedious, but still retaining the "handmade" look and a touch of nostalgia for the olden days. Good luck.

24in (61.0cm) French bisque, ball-jointed body, paperweight eyes, human hair wig, marked on head: Déposé//Tete Jumeau//Bte. S.G.D.G.//(Artist's mark in red). All original costume consists of a striped silk dress in Kate Greenaway style with tucks and featherstitch trim on skirt. The bouffant sleeves are on long cuffs with featherstitching at wrists. A softly gathered double lace collar completes the neckline. A mob-type cap of matching fabric has a very full frill of lace over a pleated brim.

13in (33.0cm) Jumeau, French bisque, closed mouth, ball-jointed body, paperweight eyes, human hair wig, marked: DÉPOSÉ//TETE JUMEAU//5 1/. Jumeau with an original striped silk dress and velvet trim.

24in (61.0cm) SPECIAL, German bisque, ball-jointed body, sleep eyes, human hair wig, marked SPECIAL//GERMANY. Doll in a pink cotton Russian-bloused dress trimmed with double shoulder ruffles of white embroidered linen, and a "beefeater" hat.

21in (53.3cm) Mascotte by Steiner, French bisque, ball-jointed body, paperweight eyes, human hair wig, marked: May & Cie Freres//MASCOTTE. French bisque of 1890 to 1901, dressed in a typical chemise with drawers of a loosely woven coarse cotton and trimming of "sleezy" colored ribbon. Dolls came in these outfits directly from the manufacturer.

LEFT: 20in (50.8cm) Long-faced Jumeau, French bisque, ball-jointed body, paperweight eyes, human hair wig, marked 9. Jumeau with shirred front and back, panels of blue silk on a blue-brocade A-line dress with a wide cummerbund of blue silk (1880s). **CENTER:** 20in (50.8cm) German bisque, ball-jointed wood and composition body, stationary eyes, human hair wig, unmarked. This doll is wearing a modified pompadour of silk with figured silk braid and a pale pink silk guimpe with a Normandy bonnet of the same period (1886). **RIGHT:** 20in (50.8cm) SFBJ, French bisque, five-piece composition body, paperweight eyes, human hair wig. SFBJ in a long waisted blue silk dress with multiple center front and center back pleating and white lace trim.

LEFT FIGURE: 18in (45.7cm) French bisque, ball-jointed wood and composition body, paperweight eyes, blonde human hair wig, marked on head "8." So-called "Portrait" Jumeau. Underwear is a linen "combination," buttons up back and has a drop seat. **RIGHT FIGURE:** 19in (48.3cm) French bisque, ball-jointed body, paperweight eyes, brown human hair wig, marked: Déposé//Tete Jumeau//Bte. S.G.D.G. Tucked drawers with lace trim are held on by drawstring at waist.

LEFT FIGURE: 18in (45.7cm) French bisque, ball-jointed wood and composition body, paperweight eyes, blonde human hair wig, marked on head "8." So-called "Portrait" Jumeau. Tucked petticoat with lace trim, on a front band, with drawstrings from side seams to center back. **RIGHT FIGURE:** 19in (48.3cm) French bisque, ball-jointed body, paperweight eyes, human hair wig, marked: Déposé//Tete Jumeau//Bte. S.G.D.G. Slip consists of a fitted bodice, with a tucked and lace-trimmed full skirt.

17in (43.2cm) German or French bisque, ball-jointed body, paperweight eyes, human hair wig, marked DEP. German bisque wearing a two-toned rose-silk dress, contrasting colors shown on some pleats, diagonal trim and cummerbund. A circular yoke is enhanced by a wide lace ruffle, and the doll wears a velvet bonet with flower trim and a matching plume.

LEFT: 24in (61.0cm) A.T. (Kramer reproduction) bisque, ball-jointed body, stationary eyes, human hair wig. A charming two-piece costume, this features a full walking skirt of peach silk with three rows of fluted self-fabric ruffles, topped by a full-bustled polonaise, the bustle extending from the center back section. A lace-covered set-in vest provides contrast and is buttoned down the front. The costume is topped by a "beefeater" hat with a turned up brim (1885). RIGHT: 25in (63.5cm) DEP German bisque ball-jointed body, sleep eyes, human hair wig, marked DEP. This simple cotton print with its satin finish has a normal waistline with a contrasting velvet sash tied in the back. Elbow-length sleeves are gathered slightly and finished with a lace ruffle. The guimpe is of English net.

LEFT: 18in (45.7cm) Portrait Jumeau, French bisque, ball-jointed body, paperweight eyes, human hair wig, marked <u>8</u>. Sheer silk blue and white checked pompadour-style dress with short sleeves over a sheer silk guimpe (1888). CENTER: 27in (68.6cm) French Fashion (DeNunez reproduction), mohair wig, stationary blue eyes, kid body, marked by DeNunez. French Fashion: adult fashion of the 1880s in two-tone pink with beige lace, bustled top over full walking skirt. RIGHT: 18in (45.7cm) RD, French bisque, ball-jointed body, paperweight eyes, human hair wig, marked RoD. RD wearing a turquoise silk pompadour dress with contrasting velvet trim (1888).

LEFT: 18in (45.7cm) K★R Pouty (Réné reproduction) bisque, ball-jointed body, stationary eyes, human hair wig, marked by Réné. Pouty wearing an A-line moss green silk dress with elaborate bustle and cummerbund. CENTER: 17in (43.2cm) German or French bisque, ball-jointed body, paperweight eyes, human hair wig, marked DEP. German bisque wearing a two-tone rose silk dress, long waisted with yoke and diagonal trim (1888). RIGHT: 19in (48.3cm) K★R 117 Pouty (Réné reproduction) bisque, ball-jointed body, stationary eyes, human hair wig, marked by Réné. Pouty wearing a chocolate brown polyester pompadour with contrasting velvet trim over a beige silk guimpe, and a mob-type bonnet (1887).

THE DELINEATOR

LEFT: 9½in (24.1cm) AM 390 German bisque, ball-jointed body, sleep eyes, human hair wig, marked: Armand Marseille// 390//A 12/ox M. Green silk coat dress in a princess style with self-fabric pleats around the skirt and beige lace trim. **CENTER:** 12in (30.5cm) German bisque, ball-jointed body, stationary eyes, human hair wig, unmarked. Beige coat dress with red trim, a cute little poke bonnet and separate cape (1877). **RIGHT:** 8½in (21.6cm) Bru (DeNunez reproduction) kid body, bisque hands, stationary eyes, marked by DeNunez. Blue silk coat dress of princess style with coat sleeves.

8924

Front View.

GIRLS' BLOUSE COSTUME

Costumes of this style are made of all varieties of suit goods, and sometimes two materials are united in the construction, the blouse being of some woolen fabric and the kilt of corduroy, velvet, etc. More frequently, however, one material is used throughout. Vivid contrasts are often introduced by the selection of bright fabrics for the plastron on the underwaist. A handsome costume of brown tricot of a soft quality has plaid velvet for the plastron and also for cuff facings. Another, made of deep navy-blue serge, has white braid arranged as in the present instance.

Pattern No. 8924 in eight sizes for girls from five to twelve years of age.

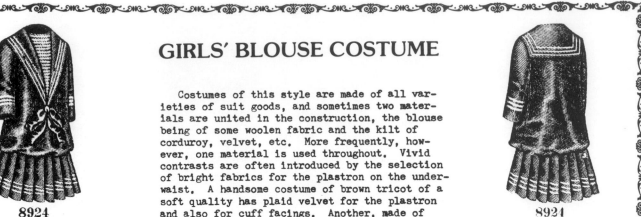

8924

Back View.

8941

Front View.

GIRLS' DRESS

Such costumes are among the prettiest of the season's modes for little women, and may be developed in any stylish woolen fabric, or in silk or velvet. Velveteen is at present much used for the costumes of little people, and is durable and rich-looking. The vest is usually in contrast with the skirt and coat, which may be alike, if preferred, and should always be of soft goods that will shirr effectively. The pattern to the costume is in eight sizes for girls from five to twelve years of age.

8941

Back View.

8921

Front View.

COSTUME FOR LITTLE GIRL

The pattern to this costume is in eight sizes for girls from five to twelve years of age. Dress goods of all varieties, silks, velvets, velveteens, cashmeres, Surahs, etc., are all suitable textures for costumes of this style, and one or more materials may be used in the construction, as preferred. Lace or embroidery may be added to the front draperies, the cape-collar and the sleeves.

8921

Back View.

14

GIRLS' COSTUME

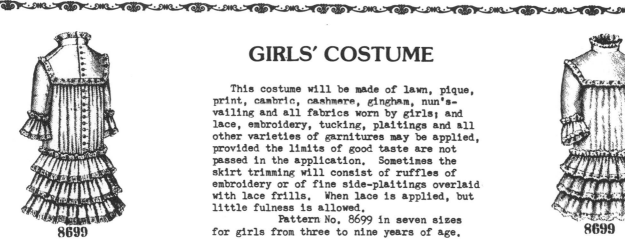

This costume will be made of lawn, pique, print, cambric, cashmere, gingham, nun's-vailing and all fabrics worn by girls; and lace, embroidery, tucking, plaitings and all other varieties of garnitures may be applied, provided the limits of good taste are not passed in the application. Sometimes the skirt trimming will consist of ruffles of embroidery or of fine side-plaitings overlaid with lace frills. When lace is applied, but little fulness is allowed.

Pattern No. 8699 in seven sizes for girls from three to nine years of age.

8699

Back View.

8699

Front View.

BACK AND FRONT VIEW OF PATTERNS SHOWN ON PRECEDING PAGE

These dresses may be made of silks, velvets, velveteens, or cashmeres, etc., with the girls' blouse costume being made of suit goods or a combination of a woolen fabric and the kilt of corduroy, velvet, etc.

1883

GIRL'S COSTUME

8920
Front View.

8920
Back View.

This costume is usually, though not necessarily, made of one variety of goods throughout, contrasting effects being, however, often introduced by the application of facings upon the vest and at the wrists of the sleeves. The skirt and vest portions may be alike and in contrast with the remainder, if desired. A pretty costume of plain and plaid suit goods has the skirt and vest portions of plain material, and the remainder of plaid goods. The skirt trimming is a narrow flounce of plaiting.

We have pattern No. 8920 in eight sizes for girls from five to twelve years of age.

1883

CHILD'S GORED DRESS

8700
Front View.

8700
Back View.

Turquoise blue cashmere, Oriental lace and insertion, and a broad sash of turquoise blue satin ribbon enter into the construction and garniture of this beautiful little costume. Also, all kinds of white goods are made up into costumes of this style and trimmed with wash laces, narrow ruffles, tiny plaitings or any other garnitures deemed appropriate. Cashmeres, nun's-vailings, ginghams, lawns, prints and all other seasonable textures adapted to children's wear will also be made up in this fashion. A pretty fancy is developed by applying colored embroideries upon white goods and vice versa.

Pattern comes in five sizes--from two to six years of age.

1883

CHILD'S COSTUME

8687
Front View.

8687
Back View.

Lawn, nainsook, print, cashmere, nun's-vailing and all materials adapted to children's dresses make up prettily in this way and may be trimmed with lace, embroidery, narrow ruffles or any other garniture preferred. A pretty dress is made of white cambric, and the lower part is ornamented with a flounce of deep embroidery headed by a row of insertion, this being in turn surmounted by a row of narrow edging. The material is cut away from beneath the flounce, and the effect is very handsome. Narrow edging and insertion trim the neck and sleeves. Star braid edging, and likewise tatting, is in good taste upon many kinds of dress goods.

We have pattern No. 8687 in seven sizes for children from six months to six years of age.

1884

GIRLS' COSTUME

9055
Front View.

9055
Back View.

The garment is as attractive as it is novel in construction and its beauty is easily developed in any material, dress goods of a plain texture, with velvet for trimming, being represented in the present instance. Another costume is of garnet cashmere throughout, and the collar is bordered with Medici lace, the sleeves being finished with lace turned back flatly from the wrists in cuff fashion.

We have pattern No. 9053 in eight sizes for girls from five to twelve years of age.

1884

COSTUME FOR GIRLS

Dress goods similar to nun's-vailing in appearance but of a firmer texture were chosen for this costume, and plaitings of the same and lace form the trimming.

Very often the ornamental front-portion of such a costume will be of Surah, silk or figured goods contrasting with the remainder of the garment, and the lower trimming will correspond. A pretty costume of plain cashmere has the ornamental portion of soft Surah, and the skirt trimming is a plaiting of cashmere faced quite deeply with Surah at the top and caught down in shell shape to disclose the facing prettily.

Pattern in eight sizes for girls from five to twelve years.

9053
Front View.

9053
Back View.

1884

GIRL'S COSTUME

This pattern is in seven sizes for girls from three to nine years of age.

The costume has some very jaunty suggestions of the sailor style and is here developed in serge. The body flares from the waist-line to the shoulders, exposing a narrow vest that is permanently attached underneath at one side and fastened with buttons and button-holes in a fly at the opposite side. Flannels, cashmeres, cloths, camel's hairs and soft woolens of all varieties make up charmingly in this way; and plaid, striped or fancy goods of any preferred variety may be used in combination, with stylish effect. Braids of all kinds, including the tinsel varieties, may be used in embellishing such costumes.

9553
Front View.

9553
Back View.

1884

GIRL'S DRESS

Such costumes as this will be made of light and dark, and thick and thin goods, according to their intended uses. Thin silks, mulls, organdies, nun's-vailings, cashmeres, Surahs, etc., will all be chosen for party wear, and lace may be added to the ornamental portions and paniers, with charming effect. For house and street wear, all varieties of woolens, also velvets, velveteens, plushes, cloths, flannels, etc., will be chosen, and may be made up singly or in combination with some pretty contrasting material. Pattern in sizes three to nine yrs.

9530
Front View.

9530
Side-Back View.

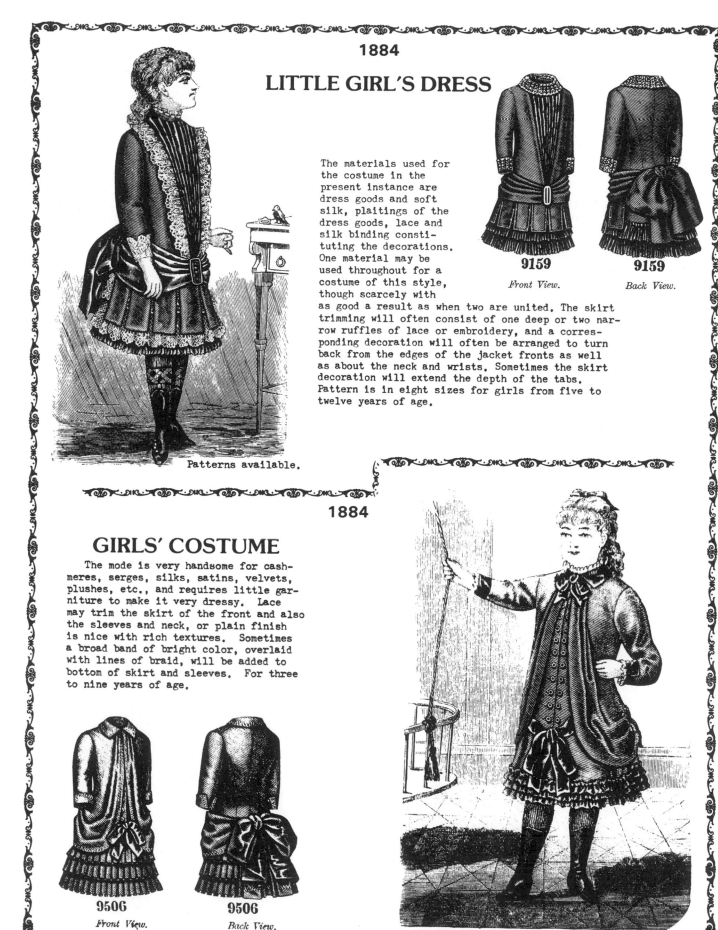

1884

LITTLE GIRL'S DRESS

The materials used for the costume in the present instance are dress goods and soft silk, plaitings of the dress goods, lace and silk binding constituting the decorations. One material may be used throughout for a costume of this style, though scarcely with as good a result as when two are united. The skirt trimming will often consist of one deep or two narrow ruffles of lace or embroidery, and a corresponding decoration will often be arranged to turn back from the edges of the jacket fronts as well as about the neck and wrists. Sometimes the skirt decoration will extend the depth of the tabs. Pattern is in eight sizes for girls from five to twelve years of age.

9159
Front View.

9159
Back View.

Patterns available.

1884

GIRLS' COSTUME

The mode is very handsome for cashmeres, serges, silks, satins, velvets, plushes, etc., and requires little garniture to make it very dressy. Lace may trim the skirt of the front and also the sleeves and neck, or plain finish is nice with rich textures. Sometimes a broad band of bright color, overlaid with lines of braid, will be added to bottom of skirt and sleeves. For three to nine years of age.

9506
Front View.

9506
Back View.

1886

LITTLE GIRLS' DRESS

This pattern is in eight sizes for girls from five to twelve. The over-dress is a novel and pretty fashion. The fronts open in V fashion toward the shoulders, and between them is visible a V-shaped vest of silk that is inserted in Breton fashion, buttons and button-holes. Fancy cuffs are simulated with the silk on the coat sleeves, and frills of lace are worn as lingerie. The vest will often be overlaid with lace net or embroidered webbing shirred into a pretty fulness at the top. Lace ruffles, plaitings or ruffles of the dress goods or of embroidery will trim the skirt stylishly, and the collar and sleeves may be likewise trimmed. Sateens, foulards, pongees, ginghams, etc., are nice with lace trim.

Front View.

Back View.

904 Patterns available.

1885

GIRLS' COSTUME

Dress goods of a summery texture were developed in the present instance, with ruffles of the same and lace for trimming. The over-dress is a prettily shaped polonaise, having jacket fronts that close with button-holes and buttons, the right side being hemmed and the left underfaced. A costume of pink nun's-vailing has three little ruffles of white lace about the bottom of the skirt. The vest is of satin overlaid with lace. Ages three to nine years.

9853
Back View.

9853
Front View.

Patterns available.

1887

CHILD'S DRESS

1372
Front View

The dress is fashioned in a style that is particularly admired on account of its youthful and dainty effect. Plain dress goods, velvet and cambric were chosen for it in this instance. There is also at present a prevailing fancy for making the dress proper of dark or neutral tinted goods and the guimpe of white goods, but if personal taste is better pleased another arrangement may be followed. Garnet, navy, seal and browns are among the preferred colors for such dresses. Sometimes the guimpe is of Surah or velvet, and sometimes of wool in contrasting color. Patterns from two to six years of age.

Patterns available.
Back View

1887

GIRL'S DRESS

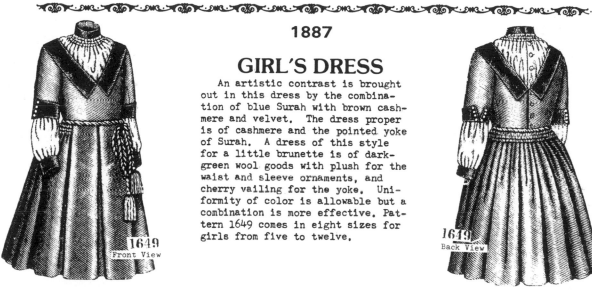

1649
Front View

An artistic contrast is brought out in this dress by the combination of blue Surah with brown cashmere and velvet. The dress proper is of cashmere and the pointed yoke of Surah. A dress of this style for a little brunette is of dark-green wool goods with plush for the waist and sleeve ornaments, and cherry vailing for the yoke. Uniformity of color is allowable but a combination is more effective. Pattern 1649 comes in eight sizes for girls from five to twelve.

1649
Back View

1887

GIRL'S COSTUME

1726
Front View.

The fashionable combination of red and black is here achieved, the red material being cashmere and the black velvet. If desired, any variety of ribbon may be used for the sash portions, but usually the dress goods will be preferred for them. If three materials are made up, the center-front and center-back portions may be of soft silk of a plain or fancy variety. Other combinations of color may be developed and any preferred choice of materials may be made.

Patterns in six sizes for children from two to seven years of age.

1726
Back View.

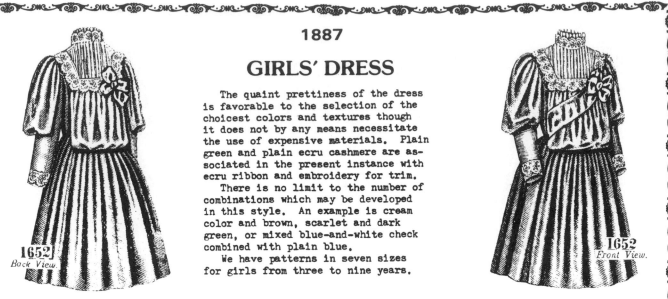

1887

GIRLS' DRESS

The quaint prettiness of the dress
is favorable to the selection of the
choicest colors and textures though
it does not by any means necessitate
the use of expensive materials. Plain
green and plain ecru cashmere are associated in the present instance with
ecru ribbon and embroidery for trim.

There is no limit to the number of
combinations which may be developed
in this style. An example is cream
color and brown, scarlet and dark
green, or mixed blue-and-white check
combined with plain blue.

We have patterns in seven sizes
for girls from three to nine years.

1652
Back View.

1652
Front View.

1887

GIRLS' DRESS

Cashmere and velvet were chosen for
this dress in the present instance, the
yoke being velvet as is the bias belt.
Dresses of this style will often have the
skirt and drapery made of embroidered
flouncing. A sash may take place of belt.
Dresses of dark wool goods will often have
the yoke, cuff facings and belt of bright
plush or cashmere or fancy figured goods.

This pattern, #1634, comes in seven
sizes for girls from three to nine years
of age.

1634 Back View.

Front View. 1631

1887

GIRLS' COSTUME

The selection of plain dress
goods and enough velvet to bring
out an effective contrast is pro-
ductive of a very pleasing result
in the present instance.

A costume of this style which is
very pretty without being at all
expensive is made of plain serge,
with plaid goods for the yoke, collar and trimming band. Another,
equally practical, is of cashmere,
with narrow braid arranged in
straight lines for decoration.

Pattern in eight sizes for girls
from five to twelve years of age.

Back View

1661
Front View

1888

GIRLS' DRESS

This mode will develop particularly well in combinations of materials and colors, and with the pretty flowered and figured goods in vogue some very unique and picturesque effects may be realized.

Braids, cordings, pipings, fancy stitchings, etc., are favored trimmings, and on serviceable costumes wide braid will frequently be arranged as the ribbons in this instance. A dainty dress made up by this fashion is of shell-pink Surah and point d' esprit net, with ruby velvet ribbon and lace edging for garnitures. Another is cardinal Surah and baby-blue crepe. Pattern comes in five sizes for girls from three to seven years of age.

2345   2345

Patterns available.

1888

GIRLS' COSTUME

A combination is usually preferred for this garment as it brings out the guimpe effect to best advantage. Cashmere, camel's-hair, foule, plaid or plain serge, etc., are favored, and with any of them cashmere, nun's-vailing or silk in any contrasting color may be used. Lace, embroidery, etc. are pretty decorations. A silk sash may be worn. Pale-pink albatross and white China silk with Genoese point lace for trimming are nice.

2265
Front View.

2265
Back View.

Patterns available.

1889

GIRLS' DIRECTOIRE COSTUME

In the present instance the costume is shown developed in green cashmere, green-and-absinthe striped Surah, and velvet to match the green stripe, with velvet and Persian bands for garnitures.

The mode will develop nicely in a single material, but combinations are more effective. The costume is suitable for almost any occasion, being sufficiently dressy to be worn when dainty dresses of silk or tulle are generally chosen.

The pattern is in eight sizes for girls from five to twelve years of age.

Back View. 2682

2682 *Front View.*

1889

GIRLS' DRESS

This simple little costume is pictured made of hemstitched embroidered flouncing, plain nainsook and solid embroidery. Combinations of materials will make up well in a dress of this kind. Chambrays, figured and plain batistes, zephyrs, lawns, summer silks, etc. will develop well in this way, the jacket, cuffs and collar always being of the fancy material.

The pattern comes in eight sizes for girls from five to twelve years of age.

Back View. 2638

2638 *Front View.*

1889

BLOUSE COSTUME

This pattern is in eight sizes for girls from five to twelve years of age.

Dark-blue serge is pictured here, with plaid and white goods, ribbon and fancy stitching for decoration.

Challis, cashmere, etc., and figured goods, will develop well. Many varities of cotton materials will also make up well in this way, and combinations may be made using contrasting textures or colors. Braids, ribbons, and fancy stitching are the most popular garnitures. The broad sash may be of ribbon, and the vest, collar and cuffs embroidered with silver or gold soutache.

Back View. 2679

2679 *Front View.*

1889

LITTLE GIRLS' DRESS

Bordered dress goods were chosen for the dress in this instance, with cuff facings of the material and ribbon for decoration. Soft textured fabrics such as camelette, nun's-vailing and embroidered cashmere will also make up nicely with ribbon or braid for garniture. Spun wash silks, foulards, etc., will make up well and they may be trimmed with lace if desired.

Pattern is in six sizes for girls from two to seven years of age.

2709
Front View.

2709
Back View.

1889

GIRLS' OUTDOOR TOILETTES.

No. 2683

No. 2679

No. 2682

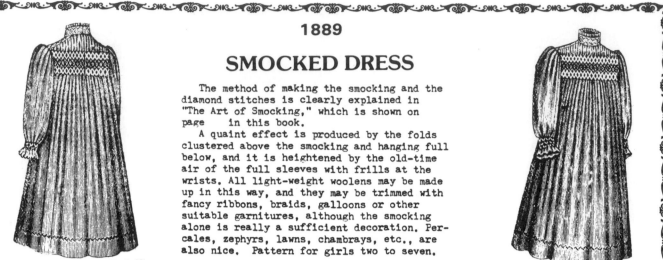

1889

SMOCKED DRESS

The method of making the smocking and the diamond stitches is clearly explained in "The Art of Smocking," which is shown on page   in this book.

A quaint effect is produced by the folds clustered above the smocking and hanging full below, and it is heightened by the old-time air of the full sleeves with frills at the wrists. All light-weight woolens may be made up in this way, and they may be trimmed with fancy ribbons, braids, galloons or other suitable garnitures, although the smocking alone is really a sufficient decoration. Percales, zephyrs, lawns, chambrays, etc., are also nice. Pattern for girls two to seven.

2666   *Back View.*

Front View. 2666

1889

LITTLE GIRLS' DRESS

Nun's-vailing, China silk, challis, spun wash silk, etc., will develop well by the mode; and any desired combination of color or texture may be achieved. The high-necked waist may be of nainsook, with a decoration of lace insertion or embroidery. For serge, cashmere, etc., the most appropriate garnitures are fancy stitching, braid and moire or fancy-edged ribbon. Lace will trim sheer fabrics prettily.

2671   *Back View.*

Front View. 2671

1889

LITTLE GIRL'S APRON

The apron may be seen developed in white nainsook, with embroidered insertion and edging for trimming.

With aprons of this kind many little dresses that otherwise would not be presentable may be utilized. For school wear the apron is a complete protection to the gown, and when daintily made will look very much like a pretty over-dress. Any sort of white washable goods will develop well in this way, and lace, colored embroidery, crochetted edging or a simple ruffle of the material may provide the decoration. Ginghams, chambrays and colored linens are frequently chosen.

Pattern comes in seven sizes for girls from two to eight years of age.

2655
Back View.

2655
Front View.

1889

LITTLE GIRLS' DRESS
(In the Gretchen Style)

Simple dresses of this kind will make up nicely for summer wear in any light fabrics. For chambrays, lawns, ginghams and other cotton fabrics the mode is an especial favorite. The yokes may be of tucking, embroidery or lace. A dress of navy-blue gingham may have the yokes of Turkey-red, trimmed with blue embroidery. We have patterns in four sizes for little girls from two to five years of age.

2663
Front View.

Back View.

1889

CHILD'S SLIP

These slips are rarely completed with great elaboration, but a dainty effect may be achieved by finishing the hem with feather, vine or other fancy stitching. All kinds of white goods in cotton and linen are desirable for them, and so are cambrics, nainsooks, lace-striped piqués, muslins. Light-weight woolens are also adaptable to the mode. Patterns come in seven sizes for children from six months to six years of age.

2640
Front View.

Back View.

1889

No. 2655   No. 2640   No. 2671   No. 2666

1890

LITTLE GIRLS' DRESS

The mode may be attractively developed in a single material; all sorts of dress goods, especially the soft woolens, such as cashmere, Henrietta cloth, challis, nun's-vailing, etc., will make up prettily in this way, and velvet or silk will unite effectively with any of them. Velvet, moire, grosgrain or satin ribbon may provide the decoration. A dainty dress may combine sapphire-blue velvet and cream Surah in its construction, and several rows of feather-stitching done with silk to match the velvet may decorate the skirt above the edge.

We have pattern No. 3446 in five sizes for girls from two to six years of age.

3446
Back View.

3446
Front View.

1890

LITTLE GIRLS' DRESS
(Also Known As The Red Riding Hood Frock)

The mode will develop prettily in cashmere, serge, challis and other wool materials combined with velvet, Surah, silk, etc. Gingham, percale and all seasonable fabrics will also make attractive dresses of this kind, and lace, embroidery, fancy braid, galloon, ribbon, etc., in any pretty color may form the decoration.

3435 *Back View.*

Front View. 3435

1890

GIRLS' COSTUME

The dress is especially adaptable to combinations and will develop prettily in all sorts of woolen or soft silken fabrics, such as cashmere, camel's-hair, foule, all-wool Surah, nun's-vailing, Henrietta cloth, China, India or Surah silk, etc. Velvet or silk will unite well with woolen fabrics.

We have this pattern in six sizes for girls from two to seven years of age.

3440 *Back View.*

Front View. 3440

1890

BLOUSED DRESS

Pink-and-gray striped French flannel and velvet are pictured in this dress. Cashmere, serge, foule, gingham or any seasonable material may be employed for a dress of this kind, and lace, embroidery, velvet ribbon, feather-stitching or braid may be used in any pretty way for garniture.

We have patterns in six sizes for girls from three to eight years of age.

3451
Front View.

3451
Back View.

1890

SMOCKED DRESS

See page 99 for smocking instructions taken from the Delineator.

Cashmere, flannel, Henrietta cloth and all soft woolens will make charming little dresses of this kind, and the mode is especially well adapted to Surah, India or China silk, foulard, etc., to which many dainty garnitures of fancy stitching in contrasting colors, ribbon, braid, etc., may be added.

The dress hangs free from the smocking and is encircled at the waist by a broad sash that is widely hemmed at the ends and tied in a bow at the back. Patterns come in nine sizes for girls from one to nine years of age.

FIGURE NO. 417 L.—LITTLE GIRLS' DRESS.—This illustrates Pattern No. 3432

3432
Front View.

3432
Back View.

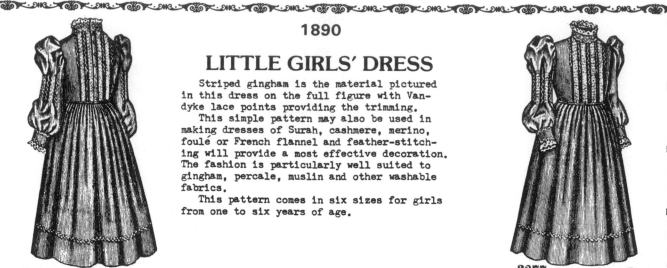

1890

LITTLE GIRLS' DRESS

Striped gingham is the material pictured in this dress on the full figure with Vandyke lace points providing the trimming.

This simple pattern may also be used in making dresses of Surah, cashmere, merino, foulé or French flannel and feather-stitching will provide a most effective decoration. The fashion is particularly well suited to gingham, percale, muslin and other washable fabrics.

This pattern comes in six sizes for girls from one to six years of age.

Back View. **3277**

3277 *Front View.*

1890

CHILD'S DRESS

The dress here pictured made of chambray and all-over embroidery, trimmed with white embroidered edging and feather-stitching, has a full round skirt which is finished with a deep hem at the bottom, above which it is artistically decorated with feather-stitching in the form of interlinked rings. The dress is simple of construction and may be developed in all sorts of dress goods of either woolen or cotton texture. Seersucker, lawn, gingham, muslin, embroidered flouncing, etc., will generally be selected for a dress of this kind.

Pattern is in six sizes for little girls from one to six years of age.

Back View. **3267**

3267 *Front View.*

1890

DRESS FOR LITTLE GIRLS

This mode will develop beautifully in sheer fabrics, and also in China, India and Surah silks and all kinds of soft woolens. A wide sash or a narrow ribbon may be arranged about the waist and tied in long loops and ends at the back. A very dainty dress for a little girl is of India silk of pale-blue and Irish-point lace. The hem of the full skirt is held in place with white floss in a pretty briar pattern, and the wrists are covered with Irish-point lace.

The pattern comes in six sizes for girls from three to eight years of age.

Back View. **3268**

3268 *Front View.*

LITTLE GIRLS' DRESS AND BONNET

The dress pattern, No. 3260, is in six sizes for girls from three to eight years of age.

The dress will develop prettily in nainsook, muslin and pique, and more serviceably in gingham, seersucker, chambray, percale and a large variety of seasonable woolens. The V shape may be overlaid with rows of insertion and novelty bands or faced with all-over embroidery velvet or silk; and the cut-away edges may be outlined with lace frills, fancy stitching, ribbon or other suitable trimmings. The bonnet may be of velvet, armure, Surah, a soft woolen fabric or a combination of two harmonizing textures or colors; and it will be trimmed with laces, braiding, embroideries, fancy cords, bows of silk or ribbon, etc., according to taste.

3260
Front View.

3260
Back View.

No. 3268

No. 3277

No. 3267

No. 3261

1892

LITTLE GIRLS' DRESS
With Medium-Short Waist

4786
Front View.

4786
Back View.

This pretty little dress, so simple in construction yet so dainty in effect, is here pictured made of light-green cashmere and tastefully decorated with fancy stitching. The full, gathered skirt hangs in free, graceful folds from a medium-short waist, and the bottom is finished with a deep hem which is held in position by a single row of fancy stitching wrought with white embroidery silk. Such little gowns will develop nicely in plain and figured India silk, Surah, crepon, cashmere, serge, camel's-hair, challis or merino and may be trimmed with bands of velvet, moiré ribbon, gimp, etc. Ribbon passed around the waist and bowed at the back will be very stylish.

Pattern comes in nine sizes for little girls from one-half to eight years of age.

. No. 4786

1892

CHILD'S DRESS
(Also Known As The Gretchen Dress)

This pattern is in seven sizes for children from one-half to six years of age.

The little dress is fashioned in the quaint Gretchen style and is here pictured made of Faience-blue India silk. The full, round skirt reaches below the ankles and is decorated at its hemmed lower edge with a band of ribbon that is tied in loop-bows at intervals.

A picturesque dress may be developed by the mode in plain or figured challis, serge, cashmere, flannel, lawn, gingham, percale or any of the numerous other fashionable varieties of dress goods of woolen or cotton texture. A cashmere dress made up in this way may be rendered as fanciful as desired by the addition of lace, embroidery, feather-stitching, ribbon or fancy braid in any pretty way preferred.

4749
Front View.

4749
Back View.

No. 4749

1892

LITTLE GIRLS' COSTUME

This blouse-dress pattern is in eight sizes for girls from five to twelve years.
It is pictured here made of rose vailing. The upper part of the dress is a blouse which is shaped in low square outline at the top both front and back. The mode is suitable for either best or ordinary wear and will develop beautifully in cashmere, serge, foulé, flannel or novelty dress goods combined with Surah or China silk for the guimpe. For winter wear, the mode will make up attractively in two shades of cashmere, and dainty garniture of fancy stitching, braid, gimp or ribbon may be added for a foot trimming on the skirt.

4891
Front View.

4891
Back View.

1892

GIRLS' DRESS

4889
View without Frills.

This pattern is in eight sizes for girls from five to twelve years.
The dress is portrayed developed in Russian-green cashmere combined with velvet of a darker hue. The skirt is full and is trimmed at the bottom with a pinked frill. Material may be cashmere, serge, flannel, vicuna, vigogne, camel's-hair and other woolens of seasonable texture.

4889
Back View.

1894

LITTLE GIRLS' DRESS

The dresses for little girls that are of simple design are always popular and the one shown here is made of pearl-gray cashmere figured with ruby rings, and rich ruby-colored velvet is used for trimming. The dress may be made up with a high neck and long sleeves or with a low neck and short sleeves. The mode is well suited to cashmere, serge, vailing, silk, Fayetta and the lightweight materials that show pretty mixtures of wool and silk.

We have this pattern in eight sizes for little girls from two to nine years of age.

7254
Back View.

7254

7254
Front View

1894

CHILD'S DRESS

This pattern comes in eight sizes for children from one-half to seven years of age.

Navy-blue cashmere showing red dots was here selected to make the dress. If the Bertha frills and yoke on this little dress are omitted, perfect simplicity may be attained, as shown in the small picture. The dress will make up nicely in soft cashmere, Henrietta, veiling, crépon, challis and fancy silks or numerous washable materials.

7214
Front View.

7214

7214
Back View.

1894

LITTLE GIRL'S DRESS

The fanciful dress is here shown made of hunter's-green camel's-hair goods associated with velvet of a darker hue. The coat-shaped sleeves are supplemented by puffs that are gathered at the top and bottom and stand out with quaint effect, the numerous folds and wrinkles that result from the fullness increasing the picturesque air. If a very plain dress is preferred, the ornaments and Bertha may be omitted. Serge, cashmere, camel's-hair and novelty suitings make up nicely and velvet, silk or satin may be united with these materials. Patterns for ages three to nine years.

7240
Back View.

7240
View without Bertha and Ornaments.

7240
Front View.

1894

GIRLS' DRESS
WITH CIRCULAR SKIRT

This dress is shown made of dark-red cashmere and silk and decorated with fancy braid. It can be made up in cashmere, serge, crepon, Henrietta, vicuna, canvas wool weaves, plaid goods and some fancy silks. Braid, velvet ribbon, gimp or galloon would be nice on wool and, on silk, ribbon or lace. Pattern in eight sizes for ages five to twelve.

7211
Back View.

7211
Front View.

View without Bretelles and Belt.

GIRLS' DRESS
WITH CIRCULAR SKIRT

The dress is here shown developed in tan-colored vicuna and dark-brown velvet. A band of velvet outlines the lower edge of the puff, imparting a neat and decorative finish. Over the shoulders, falling in ripples, are gathered bretelles that are trimmed along their free edges with velvet. The bretelles may be omitted and the dress made with a low neck and short sleeves for dressy wear.
Pattern comes in eight sizes for girls from five to twelve.

7237
Back View.

7237
Front View.

1894

GIRLS' DRESS

Dressy toilettes for girls will be made up in this manner of heliotrope, lavender, blue, pink, red or lemon-colored silk that may be figured or flowered, or the pretty checked or striped silks or those that are plain yet have changeable hues that give them charm may be chosen. Primrose-yellow crepon with black velvet ribbon is nice; delicate pink or blue tints with darker ribbon may be used for a blonde. This pattern comes in seven sizes for girls from three to nine years of age.

7205
Back View.

7205
Front View.

1895

LITTLE GIRLS' DRESS

The dress is both simple and practical, and is here pictured made of blue-and-white hair-striped gingham and decorated with embroidered edging and insertion. The small engraving shows the simplicity of the dress with the Bertha frills omitted. The dress may be made from gazine, cambric, batiste, chambray, shirred, striped and plain lawn, challis, dimity or percale. Pattern in sizes for one-half to eight years.

Back View **7621**

7621

7621 Front View

1895

GIRLS' FROCK

Pretty little dresses for wee women may be developed in percale, gingham, lawn, nainsook flouncing, batiste, etc., and in such seasonable woolens as challis, vailing, cashmere and flannel. The tabs may be of contrasting material, if desired, or may be decorated with lace insertion, braid or ribbon, the collar and sleeves being trimmed to correspond. One-half to eight yrs.

Back View **7623**

7623

7623 Front View

1895

LITTLE GIRLS' TOILETTE

This simply styled dress is shown here in lavender-and-white striped gingham and is trimmed with embroidered edging. It may be worn with or without a guimpe. Dainty washable dresses will be made of Japanese cotton crepe, gazine, chambray, batiste, dimity, lawn or organdy. We have pattern in eight sizes for girls from one to eight years of age.

Back View **7628**

7628

7628 Front View

36

1895

LITTLE GIRLS' DRESS

7615
Front View.

For the present development of the dress white crepon was chosen, with lace insertion and baby ribbon for decoration. The straight, full skirt extends to a becoming depth and is deeply hemmed at the bottom.

The little dress is especially adapted to challis, cashmere, flannel, gingham, percale, chambray, etc., and the best effect will be obtained if some contrasting material is used for the yoke.

We have this pattern in eight sizes for little girls from two to nine years of age

7615
Back View.

No. 7615

No. 7593

No. 7621

1897

GIRLS' BLOUSE DRESS

This dress is simply but prettily designed and is pictured made up in gray wool goods and decorated with lace edging and soutache braid.

The dress is adapted to silk or soft woolens, plain, checked or plaided, and may be made fanciful by bands of lace insertion, frills of edging or ribbon or rows of baby ribbon.

We have this pattern in ten sizes for girls from three to twelve years of age.

9365
Front View.

9365
Back View.

1897

GIRLS' AFTERNOON DRESS

This pattern is in eight sizes for girls from five to twelve years of age.

This frock is shown in a combination of plaid wool goods, velvet and silk. The five-gored skirt is gathered at the back and hangs from the waist, which is closed at the back. Leaf-shaped caps edged with lace add to the ornamental effect; they spread over short puffs arranged at the top of the coat-shaped sleeves, which are lace-trimmed at the wrist. This combination is much admired for girls' afternoon or best dresses. The plain materials combined with the plaid may be silk, satin, velvet or cloth and they should match the ground color of the plaid. Lace edging and insertion in cream or ecru tints and ribbon in a pretty harmonizing shade will give the finish necessary to a dressy effect.

9363
Front View.

9363
Back View.

LITTLE GIRLS' RUSSIAN BLOUSE-DRESS

A stylish frock in the favored Russian style is here represented made of golden brown camel's-hair and decorated with narrow dark-brown braid. The body is made with a lining fitted by under-arm and shoulder seams and is closed at the left side of the front in Russian fashion; it has pretty fulness drawn to the center in gathers at the neck, both front and back, and is gathered all round at the bottom and tacked to the lining to droop in blouse style over an applied belt.

Very attractive little dresses of this style may be made of serge, flannel, cashmere, Henrietta, camel's-hair and mohair, and velvet or satin ribbon will make a suitable trim.

This pattern is in eight sizes for two to nine years of age.

9498
Front View.

9498
Back View.

CHILD'S DRESS.
(To Be Made With High Or Square Neck And With Full-Length Or Short Puff Sleeves.)

This illustrates a child's dress. The pattern is in six sizes for children from one to six years old.

The simple little dress is very attractive as here made of checked gray wool goods and trimmed with red velvet ribbon. The rather long, full skirt hangs from a short plain body that is closed at the back and finished with a standing collar. A fluffy effect is given by gathered bretelles that are wide on the shoulders and taper almost to points at the ends, which terminate just above an applied belt. The close sleeves are made with short puffs at the top.

Pretty dresses for afternoon wear may be made up after this pattern in soft woolens, such as cashmere, serge and Henrietta, with lace ribbon, lace, insertion or braid for trimming.

9518
Front View.

9518

9518
Back View.

1897

GIRLS' FRENCH SAILOR COSTUME
With Four-Gored Skirt Sewed To Sleeveless Waist

This costume is well adapted for wear in the country, at the sea-shore, and for outdoor sports. It is here shown made of green serge trimmed with narrow braid. Flannel and serge are the most satisfactory materials for this style. It may also be made up in pique, flannel, linen, etc. Narrow braid, lace or Hamburg edging will provide an effective decoration. Pattern is in eight sizes for girls from five to twelve years of age.

Back View. **9167**

9167

9167 Front View

1897

GIRLS' SUMMER TOILETTE

This consists of a girls' two-piece costume and shirt-waist. The jacket and skirt are here pictured made of grey poplin and prettily trimmed with frogs and narrow soutache braid fancifully disposed. A braid-trimmed belt of the material encircles the waist. Serge, cheviot, alpaca and goods of similar weave will be chosen for the jacket and skirt, and lawn dimity, gingham and various cotton goods for the shirt-waist. For summer use linen, Russian crash, pique and duck are suitable. The fancy straw hat is trimmed with ribbon and flowers.

Pattern is in nine sizes for girls from four to twelve years of age.

9163
Front View.

9163
Back View.

9163

1897

LITTLE GIRLS' DRESS

The square neck is outlined with three rows of the ribbon and four rows decorate the standing collar, which completes the neck.

Silk, challis, serge, fine French flannel or any other pretty material suitable for children's dresses will develop this mode nicely and fancy braid, ruffles or plaitings of silk or ribbon will be appropriate for trimming.

This pattern is in six sizes for little girls from two to seven years old.

9384
Front View.

9384
Back View.

1897

CHILD'S DRESS, WITH BOLEROS

This pattern is in seven sizes for children from one to seven years.

Cashmere in any of the delicate shades becoming to the young will give great satisfaction made up in this way, and so will serge, flannel, novelty goods and, for best wear, silk. Velvet would combine with almost any material, and braid is nice. Some wee woman will appear well dressed in a gown of old-rose drap d'été made with boleros of velvet in the same or a darker tone.

9361
Front View.

9361

9361
Back View.

1897

GIRLS' DRESS, WITH FOUR-GORED SKIRT

(To Be Made With Or Without The Fancy Collarette.)

The stylish dress here illustrated is made in a pretty shade of spotted woolen dress goods of a soft weave, with silk plaitings and ribbon for decoration. Taffeta, cashmere, canvas, zibeline, mohair, serge and novelty goods are some materials in vogue for dresses of this style. Velvet, satin or corded silk could be used for the collarette. Pattern is in eight sizes for girls from five to twelve years of age.

9404

9404 *Front View.*

9404 *Back View.*

1898

LITTLE GIRLS' DRESS WITHOUT BODY LINING, (To be Worn With or Without a Guimpe.)

9994
Front View.

The dress is here portrayed made of white nainsook in combination with nainsook embroidered edging and insertion. Dotted and plain Swiss, nainsook, dimity, organdy, fine lawn or cambric, challis and vailing will be pretty for this dress, and ribbon-run beading, embroidered or lace edging and insertion will trim it daintily. This pattern is in seven sizes for girls from two to eight.

9994

9994
Back View.

Styles for Little Folks.

LITTLE GIRLS' DRESS (To be Worn With or Without a Guimpe.)

9957
Back View

Front View. **9957**

This dainty dress of lawn is fancifully trimmed with lace edging and ribbons and a guimpe, also of lawn, has a decoration of fine embroidered insertion and edging. The waist has gathered fulness in the front and backs and blouses slightly. Double frill caps spread over short puff sleeves and add to the fluffy effect. The straight skirt is gathered and joined to the body; it is trimmed above the hem with frills of edging and rows of narrow ribbon. A yoke effect is produced in the guimpe by the arrangement of tucks and insertion, and the neck and full sleeves are finished with bands of insertion bordered with frills of edging. Organdy, Swiss, chambray, dimity, batiste and zephyr gingham are fabrics suited to the dress, with guimpe of mull or India silk. The hat is prettily trimmed with lace, flowers and ribbon.

1899

GIRLS' DRESS WITH YOKE
Fitted Band And A Circular Skirt

In this instance white taffeta overlaid with lace was employed for the yoke and collar of the pale pink cashmere dress here shown, narrow black ribbon and cut crystal buttons providing the decoration. For chilly days at the seaside a pretty little dress may be made up using fawn cloth combined with blue silk for the yoke and collar and trimmed with white lace applique. Plain and figured organdy may be used with pleasing results, and the yoke, fitted band and sleeves trimmed with bands of insertion.

2756
Front View.

2756

2756
Back View.

1899

GIRLS' BLOUSE DRESS
With Four-Gored Skirt

The pretty dress here shown for a small lassie is made of pale-blue cashmere and decorated with narrow black velvet ribbon. A combination of white and pink pique will also pleasingly develop the design, which may then be decorated with white cotton braid and completed by a pink ribbon stock and sash.

This pattern is in eight sizes for girls from five to twelve years of age.

2790
Front View.

2790
Back View.

1899

GIRLS' DRESS,
With Straight Full Skirt.

This frock is very pleasing as here pictured made up in organdy trimmed with ruchings of narrow ribbon and lace frills. Dimity, lawn and fine zephyr gingham in plaids, checks and the lacy striped effects that are shown this season will make up charmingly in this frock, with ruchings of lace, bands of insertion and frills of edging to match for garniture.

This pattern is in eight sizes for girls from five to twelve years of age.

2724
Front View.

2724

2724
Back View.

1899

LITTLE GIRLS' DRESS, WITH SHORT BODY AND STRAIGHT, FULL SKIRT.

(Known As The Toddlekins Frock.)

This quaint dress, which is known as the toddlekins frock, is shown daintily developed in red cashmere with white silk for the yoke and satin ribbon for the sash. Lace frills and ruchings of ribbon provide the garniture. India silk, Swiss, organdy and lawn are appropriate for the frock, with lace insertion and edging for ornamentation. If desired, the skirt may be hemstitched.

This pattern is in six sizes for little girls from two to seven years of age.

Pattern available.

2757
Front View.

2757
Back View.

1899

CHILD'S SHIRRED DRESS IN CARTER STYLE
(To be Made with High or Open Neck and Full-Length or Short Puff Sleeves.)

Pink China silk was chosen for this little dress, which is in Carter style, and lace edging provides the decoration. The full-length sleeves are gathered at top and bottom and finished with wristbands, but, if preferred, they may be displaced by short puff sleeves over smooth linings. The dress may also be made of organdy or fine lawn. The pattern is in five sizes for children from two to six years of age.

2722
Front View.

2722
Back View.

1899

LITTLE GIRLS' DRESS

Bretelle frills of white embroidery characterize this little dress, which is shown made of plaid gingham trimmed with frills of narrow embroidery. The straight full skirt is joined to the waist with a cording. Bretelle frills that taper almost to points at their ends are arranged on the waist and ripple stylishly over the gathered tops of the one-piece sleeves. The sleeves are gathered at their lower edges and finished by narrow wristbands. Pattern is in eight sizes for little girls from two to nine years of age.

2768
Front View.

2768
Back View.

BONNETS AND HATS
shown in
DELINEATORS
1880s-1890s

MISSES' CHEMISES, and DRAWERS, COMBINED

No. 8688.--The superiority of
patterns combining as far as
possible the articles of underwear which were once constructed
separately, is now so thoroughly appreciated that, with the changes
in the styles of dresses or costumes, a corresponding adaptation is
looked for in the combination garments, and Fashion always gratifies
the expectation. The latest pattern for a child's underwaist and
drawers combines these garments in a most satisfactory manner. It
is here developed in bleached muslin and trimmed in a neat and
simple manner with embroidered edging, tucks and narrow bands of
the material. Each half of the front of the waist and the corresponding drawers leg are cut in one piece, the drawers portion
being seamless at the outside of the leg and the edges being joined
in a curving seam at the inside, there being also a seam at the center
of the back. A shapely seam, extending from the neck to the leg
seams of the drawers, adjusts the front of the waist; and the back of
this portion is joined by seams upon the shoulders and under the
arms, and is just deep enough to extend a little beneath the top of

1883

Please note that sizes from the
old DELINEATOR magazines range
in size as follows:

Children Girls	2-12 years
Misses	8-15 years

the drawers portion. The latter
is scantily gathered and is sewed
to a belt. Before the belt is
added, however, a lengthwise
slash, extending several inches
from the top, is made in each
side, and the back edge is completed with a lap. A buttonhole is worked in each end of
the belt, and corresponding buttons are sewed upon the waist.
Buttons and button-holes also
close the waist, the closing edges
being slightly curved and un-
der-faced. The pattern is cut
high in the neck, as shown by
the back view, and is perforated
to indicate the Pompadour shape.
With either outline the finish is
a row of edging set on under a
tiny band of the material. The
sleeves are short and are prettily

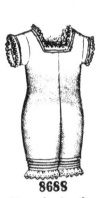

8688

*Front View, showing the neck in
Pompadour shape.*

9002

*Back View, showing the Garment
with a High Neck and Full-
Length Sleeves.*

9002

*Front View, showing the Garment
with a Low, Round Neck and
Short Sleeves.*

shaped, each consisting of a single piece. The finish is the same a
for the neck. A row of wider edging, surmounted by a cluster of
fine tucks, trims the drawers prettily at the lower edge.

Cambric or any material used for such garments makes up satisfactorily in this way and may be trimmed in any manner to please
the fancy. The neck is cut out or left high, according to the health
of the little wearer and the style of the outside clothing. Torchon
lace is much liked for trimming
cambric and fine muslin, and so
are nainsook, embroidery and
fine edgings. For delicate children, these garments are often
made of thin flannel to wear
under duplicate cotton garments.

We have pattern No. 8688 in
five sizes for children from two
to six years of age. For a child
of six years, it will require two
yards of material twenty-seven
inches wide, or one yard and
three-fourths thirty-six inches
wide.

8688

Back View, showing a High Neck.

Any material in vogue for
underwear may be made up in
this fashion, muslin being perhaps more popular than any
other texture. The question,
"what kind of muslin is the best
for general wear," is often asked,
and, while no special brand can
be credited with possessing all
the advantages that another has
not, it may be said in reply that
a quality having a flat warp, not
too closely woven, is likely to
give the best satisfaction in a
general sense, though it has not the smooth, even appearance of
some textures. The trimming may be of any kind admired, but it
is well to remember that decoration of any kind does not wear as
well as the material, and that simple garnitures are best adapted to
garments intended for frequent use. The wearing qualities of lace,
Hamburg edging, etc., are increased by a reasonable amount of fulness in the sewing on.

We have pattern No. 9002 in eight sizes for misses from eight to
fifteen years of age.

1878

6405
Front View.

6405
Back View.

MISSES' COMBINATION CHEMISE, CORSET-COVER AND UNDER-SKIRT.

1883
GIRLS' UNDERWAIST
and
PETTICOAT COMBINED

8714

Front View, showing the Garment with Low, Square Neck and without Sleeves.

8714

Back View, showing the Garment with High Neck and Coat Sleeves.

No. 8714.--The method of combining two undergarments in one, which this pattern illustrates, obtains now almost entirely in the preparation of girls' wardrobes, having been found much more comfortable and convenient than the old fashion of making each garment separately. Bleached muslin is the material represented in the garment here illustrated, and tucks, narrow wash laces and gathered ruffles form the trimming. The front is in one length from the throat to the lower edge, and is fitted by gores reaching to the shoulders, that are symmetrically curved to the figure. The body portion of the back extends only far enough below the waist-line to give a smooth adjustment about the hips, and is fitted by side-back seams that meet those of the front at the shoulders. Buttons and button-holes perform the closing, the right edge being hemmed and the left underfaced. To the lower edge is joined a skirt portion, which is gathered at the top and sewed at the sides to the adjoining edges of the side-front gores.

This arrangement provides ample width for the lower part of the garment. A narrow ruffle, bordered with lace at its lower edge, finishes the bottom of the garment very prettily. The neck is cut high, as shown in the back view; and the low, square-necked outline is obtained by cutting it out at perforations in the pattern. Either style of neck is finished with a ruffle of lace. Full-length coat sleeves are also included in the pattern, and these are usually retained with the high neck, an edging of lace at the wrists finishing them prettily. When the low-necked style is preferred, the sleeves are usually omitted and the arms'-eyes are simply finished with frills of lace or whatever trimming is used. Lonsdale cambric, percale, flannel and all other textures in use for girls' underwear are made up in this way and trimmed with ruffling, rick-rack, star braid, embroidery, etc. The provision for the high neck and long sleeves indicates the suitability of the pattern for Winter as well as for Summer fabrics.

We have pattern No. 8714 in eight sizes for girls from two to nine years of age. For a girl of eight years, the high-necked garment with sleeves will require one yard and three-fourths of material thirty-six inches wide, while the low-necked garment without sleeves will need one yard and a-half of goods in the same width.

9982
Front View

1898

9982
Back View.

DRAWERS
These Styles Span The 1880s And 1890s Showing Variations As Pictured In Old Catalogs

Extra good value muslin drawers, made with wide flounce, insertion of torchon lace. Open or closed style. A regular 50-cent drawers. Our price...25c
If by mail, postage extra, 8 cents.

When we quote open and closed style be sure and state style desired; otherwise we will send open style, which are more in demand.

A fine grade of muslin drawers, with four rows of tucks, 3-inch fine embroidery ruffle. Exceptionally good value. Open style only. Price...42c
If by mail, postage extra, 8 cents.

Very good quality muslin drawers, wide flounce with three rows of tucks and hemstitching, insertion of torchon lace and edge to match. Extra good value. Open style only. Price...55c
If by mail, postage extra, 9 cents.

PETTICOATS

A Variety Of Petticoats
From A Catalog Of The
1880s..Complete With Prices.

Ladies' White Umbrella Skirt, 3 yards around bottom, lawn ruffle 6½ inches wide finished with open work embroidery, a regular $1.25 skirt.

Each..... $0.79
2 for...... 1.52
3 for...... 2.20

A Skirt built for wear. of a fine quality muslin, the embroidery is 10 inches wide and is headed by a cloister of five tucks. The pattern of embroidery is neat and quiet, but nevertheless rich in appearance. Realizing that there are a great many women who still want the class of reliable merchandise on the market years ago, we make a special feature of this skirt. If you want a well wearing skirt order this number. Each....... $1.20

Two for.... .... 2.30

Ladies' White Muslin Skirt, lawn ruffle 6½ inches wide, trimmed with embroidery, good width. patent facing.

Each... $0.50
2 for.... .95
3 for.... 1.40

A Pretty Skirt made of a cotton embroidery 9 inches wide 4 cloister tucks, a skirt that would be good value at $1.25 This skirt is made like the good old fashioned skirts made for wear more than for show, a good skirt for ladies' wanting value and durability.

Our special price, 82c; 2 for.................. $1.58

Muslin Skirt, umbrella style, 8 yards around bottom, lawn ruffle 6½ inches wide finished with fine linen torchon lace, a regular $1.00 skirt. Each 65; 2 for $1.25; 3 for..................... $1.85

Ladies' White Skirt made of good muslin, 3 yards wide, 2 lawn ruffles 4¼ inches wide, finished with torchon lace, 3 inches wide. Retailers ask $1.50 for goods like these.

Each 90c;
2 for $1.70;
3 for $2.50

Ladies' Fine White Skirt, 3¼ yards wide, has 9-inch lawn ruffle finished with very handsome open work embroidery; regular price $2.00.

Each; $1.25.
2 for.. 2.40
3 for.. 3.30

DOLL PATTERNS SHOWN IN DELINEATORS 1880s, 1890s

LADY DOLLS' CARRIAGE TOILETTE.

SET NO. 85.—LADY DOLLS' WRAP AND TRAINED COSTUME

1883

1894

LADY DOLLS' SET NO. 176.—CONSISTING OF A BLOUSE, SKIRT AND CAPE.

Front View.   *Back View.*   *Side-Front View.*   *Side-Back View.*   *Back View.*

LADY DOLLS' SET NO. 175.—CONSISTING OF A DRAPED SKIRT, A SHIRRED WAIST AND A DOUBLE CAPE.

1894

Front View.   *Back View.*

Front View.

Right Side-Front View.   *Left Side-Back View.*

Back View.

—LADY DOLLS' TRAVELLING TOILETTE.—

DOLL PATTERNS

FIGURE NO. 438 K.—GIRL DOLLS' FRENCH DRESS.—

GIRL DOLLS' **1894** —CONSISTING OF A DRESS AND BONNET.

Front View.　　　Back View.

GIRL DOLLS' **1894** —CONSISTING OF A FRENCH DRESS AND A JACKET.

Front View.　　　Back View.

Front View.　　　Back View.

GIRL DOLLS' **1878** —CONSISTING OF A CHEMISE DRAWERS, AND PETTICOAT.

LADY DOLLS' **1888** —CONSISTING OF A CORSET–COVER, A COMBINATION CHEMISE AND DRAWERS, AND A COMBINATION CORSET–COVER AND UNDER-SKIRT.

Front View.　　　Back View.

Front View.

Front View.　　　Back View.

Back View.

1894
—GIRL DOLLS' VISITING TOILETTE.

51

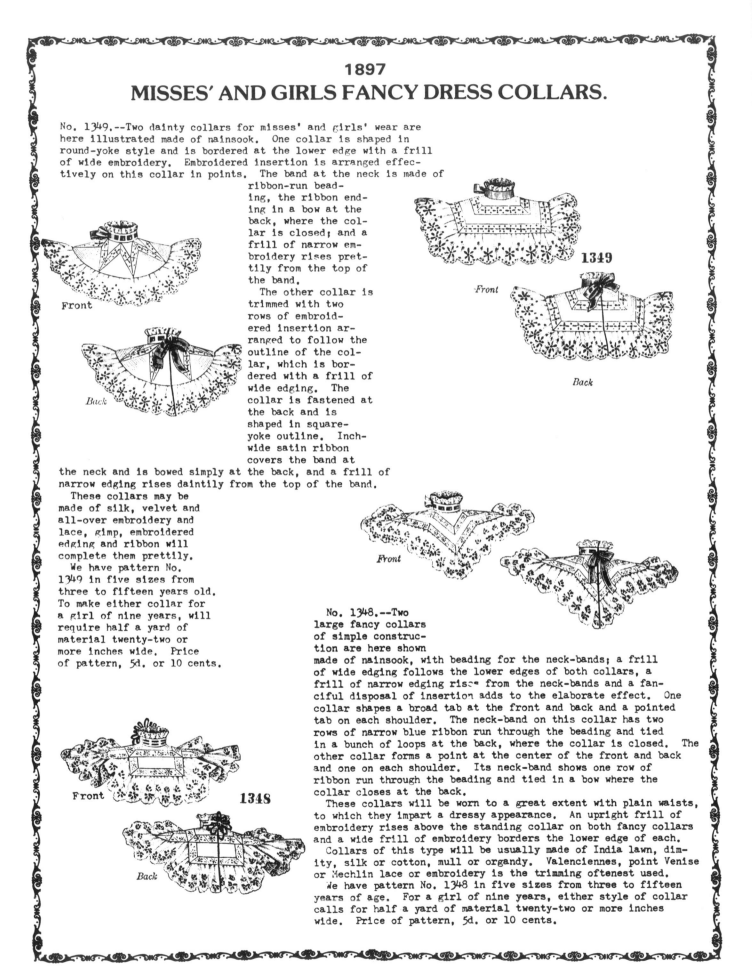

MISSES' AND GIRLS FANCY DRESS COLLARS.

No. 1349.--Two dainty collars for misses' and girls' wear are here illustrated made of nainsook. One collar is shaped in round-yoke style and is bordered at the lower edge with a frill of wide embroidery. Embroidered insertion is arranged effectively on this collar in points. The band at the neck is made of ribbon-run beading, the ribbon ending in a bow at the back, where the collar is closed; and a frill of narrow embroidery rises prettily from the top of the band.

The other collar is trimmed with two rows of embroidered insertion arranged to follow the outline of the collar, which is bordered with a frill of wide edging. The collar is fastened at the back and is shaped in square-yoke outline. Inch-wide satin ribbon covers the band at the neck and is bowed simply at the back, and a frill of narrow edging rises daintily from the top of the band.

These collars may be made of silk, velvet and all-over embroidery and lace, gimp, embroidered edging and ribbon will complete them prettily.

We have pattern No. 1349 in five sizes from three to fifteen years old. To make either collar for a girl of nine years, will require half a yard of material twenty-two or more inches wide. Price of pattern, 5d. or 10 cents.

Front

Back

1349

Front

Back

Front

No. 1348.--Two large fancy collars of simple construction are here shown made of nainsook, with beading for the neck-bands; a frill of wide edging follows the lower edges of both collars, a frill of narrow edging rises from the neck-bands and a fanciful disposal of insertion adds to the elaborate effect. One collar shapes a broad tab at the front and back and a pointed tab on each shoulder. The neck-band on this collar has two rows of narrow blue ribbon run through the beading and tied in a bunch of loops at the back, where the collar is closed. The other collar forms a point at the center of the front and back and one on each shoulder. Its neck-band shows one row of ribbon run through the beading and tied in a bow where the collar closes at the back.

These collars will be worn to a great extent with plain waists, to which they impart a dressy appearance. An upright frill of embroidery rises above the standing collar on both fancy collars and a wide frill of embroidery borders the lower edge of each.

Collars of this type will be usually made of India lawn, dimity, silk or cotton, mull or organdy. Valenciennes, point Venise or Mechlin lace or embroidery is the trimming oftenest used.

We have pattern No. 1348 in five sizes from three to fifteen years of age. For a girl of nine years, either style of collar calls for half a yard of material twenty-two or more inches wide. Price of pattern, 5d. or 10 cents.

Front

1348

Back

STYLES FOR BOYS.

1883
BOYS' JERSEY COSTUME

No. 8955.

Conspicuous among the stylish costumes for small lads is the Jersey costume, which includes a jacket, pants and cap, all made of Jersey goods. Such a costume is here represented as made of navy-blue stockinet. The pants are lined all through with Silesia and fit smoothly and closely. A deep, round collar of white linen is at the neck, and sometimes white cuffs are worn with such costumes, and a knitted scarf of Indian red with tasselled ends is tied jauntily about the waist, the ends falling at the left side. The pattern is in eight sizes for boys from three to ten years.

The cap consists of a crown that is plaited closely at the top under a plush pompom. It is lined with satin, and to it is seamed the side or brim portion, which is double and has an interlining of crinoline to stiffen it. The pattern to the cap is in eight sizes for boys from three to ten years.

1885
BOYS' SUIT

This consists of a boys' jacket and knee trousers. Both patterns are in eight sizes for boys from three to ten years of age.

This is a very neat and stylish suit for a little man, and is here shown made of fancy suiting. The jacket has its fronts reversed in lapels to the first button and button-hole, and the lapels meet a rolling collar in notches. A little back of the closing are stitched three forward-turning tucks, which extend only to a little below the waist-line. Three forward-turning tucks are stitched in each side of the back, and the lower end of the center seam is nicely rounded away. The lower front corners of the jacket are square, and all the edges are finished with a row of stitching made close to them. The trousers extend to the knees and have fancy laps inserted in the lower part of their outside leg-seams.

All kinds of suitings may be made up into very stylish patterns, and so may Cheviots, tricots, diagonals, serges, flannels, Tweeds, cloths in plain and fancy varieties, etc., and the finish may be machine-stitching or braid, or it may be perfectly plain.

The hat is a stylish Derby.

53

1885

BOYS' SAILOR SUIT

These patterns, Sailor Blouse #517 and
Trousers #9248, come in eleven sizes for boys
from five to fifteen years of age. For the
little man who goes on any sea trip, this is
a most appropriate and comfortable suit.
Flannel was employed for it in this instance
and is the material best adapted to the mode.

Soft cloths are best liked for such suits,
and braid or machine-stitching is the usual
finish for the blouse (jacket). Anchors,
stars, crosses, etc., may be embroidered in
the corners of the collars and on the vest
with pretty effect.

The cap is made of fancy cloth and has a
band of ribbon about its brim, the ends falling in short streamers in the back. The
word "Atlantic" is worked in the band, but,
of course, any other name can take its place.

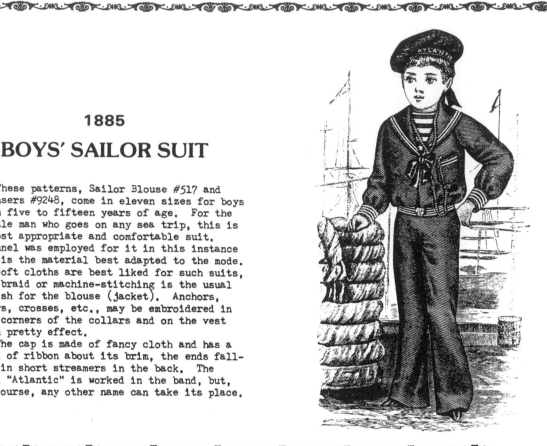

1885

LITTLE BOYS' KILT COSTUMES

These two similar little boy Kilt Suits
come in five sizes for boys two to six
years of age.

Suit #2276 is made of fancy mixed suiting with buttons and machine-stitching providing the finish. The body is inclined
to the figure by the usual shaping seams and
is joined to the skirt which is plain for
some distance in front and kilt-plaited the
rest of the way around. Figure #391A is
very similar. The skirt is made the same
way except it laps widely in front and
closes with buttons.

Materials used for both suits include
silk and wool mixtures, fancy cloths,
serges, Cheviots, and plaid or plain
cloths. Soutache braid, silk or mohair
braid may outline the edges or it may be
formed in a single coil on the skirt, collar and cuffs. Dark green or blue serge
may be trimmed with black soutache. Velvet
makes a very dressy costume with broad,
flat silk braid trimming. The stylish hat
is a Tyrolese shape in silk beaver.
Figure #391A wears a polo cap made of cloth
matching the suit.

No. 391 A   No. 2276,

LORD FAUNTLEROY SUITS.

The popularity of the Lord Fauntleroy suits is due in large part to their appearance in the characterization of a "little lord", the hero of Frances Hodgson Burnett's famous work which has been playing in London and New York.

The hero, a young boy of sunny disposition and angelic mien, appeared in four costumes, three of which are shown here -- the sailor, the riding suit and the court suit. Young boys will wear them until their ages are written in double numbers.

Suit #2572 consists of white jersey trousers, white silk Surah blouse which has a broad sailor collar of pale blue Surah. The Fauntleroy sash of the blue Surah has long fringe ends and hangs to the right side. Sizes three to twelve years.

Suit #9085 is a riding suit made of rich wine-colored corduroy with leggings of tan-colored leather and gauntlet gloves to match. The Tam O' Shanter cap is made of matching fabric although it could be knitted.

Suit #2577 is constructed of black velvet with black silk stockings and little kid slippers decorated with bows. A deep collar of Irish Point lace and deep rolling cuffs of similar lace form beautiful accessories. The waist is draped with a wide sash of crimson silk Surah. The hat is a soft felt trimmed with a bunch of ostrich tips. Sizes three to twelve years.

2572
Front View.

2572
Back View.

1985

1985

2577

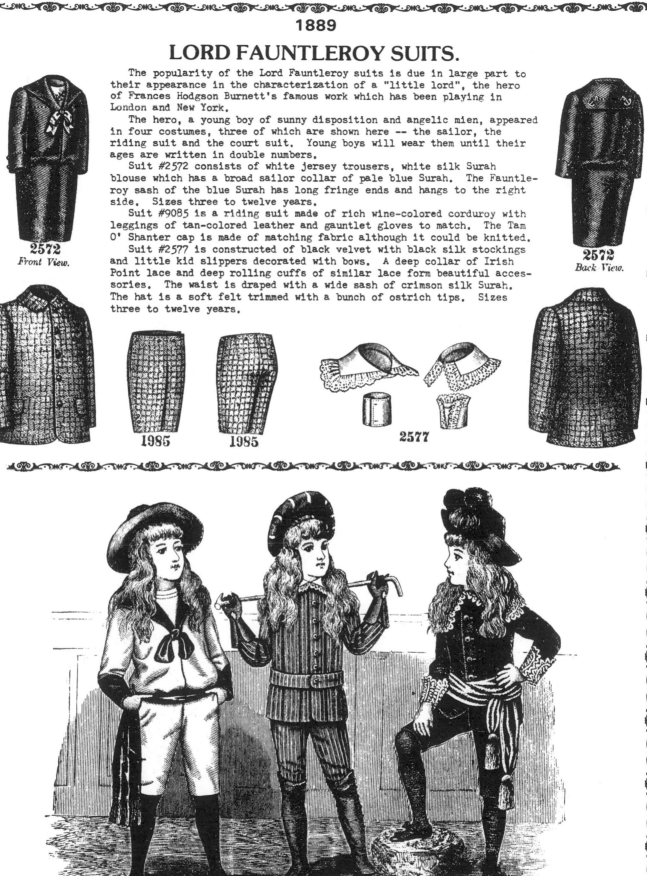

No. 2572.   No. 9085.   No. 2577.

LITTLE BOYS' COSTUME

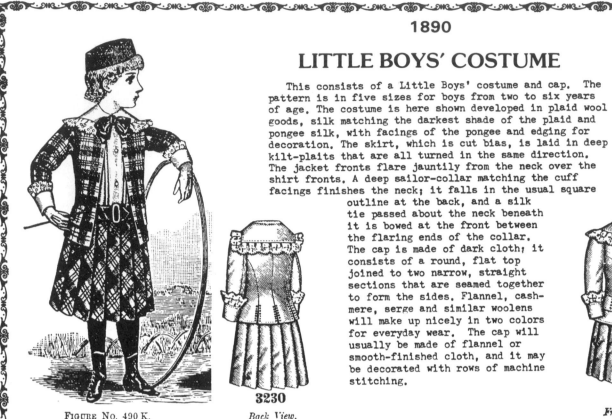

This consists of a Little Boys' costume and cap. The pattern is in five sizes for boys from two to six years of age. The costume is here shown developed in plaid wool goods, silk matching the darkest shade of the plaid and pongee silk, with facings of the pongee and edging for decoration. The skirt, which is cut bias, is laid in deep kilt-plaits that are all turned in the same direction. The jacket fronts flare jauntily from the neck over the shirt fronts. A deep sailor-collar matching the cuff facings finishes the neck; it falls in the usual square outline at the back, and a silk tie passed about the neck beneath it is bowed at the front between the flaring ends of the collar. The cap is made of dark cloth; it consists of a round, flat top joined to two narrow, straight sections that are seamed together to form the sides. Flannel, cashmere, serge and similar woolens will make up nicely in two colors for everyday wear. The cap will usually be made of flannel or smooth-finished cloth, and it may be decorated with rows of machine stitching.

FIGURE NO. 490 K.

3230
Back View.

3230
Front View.

LITTLE BOYS' REEFER JACKET
(To be Worn with Kilts and Sailor Suits)

3229
Front View.

3229
Back View.

In the present instance the jacket is shown developed in navy-blue flannel and trimmed with narrow black braid and buttons. The fronts are closed in double-breasted fashion with buttons and button-holes. At the neck is a sailor collar that presents the regulation square outline at the back; the free edges are finished with stitching, above which four rows of braid are applied. As the title suggests, the jacket is especially designed to accompany kilts and sailor suits, although it may be satisfactorily worn with other suits. Flannel, cloth, serge, checked cloths, etc., are adaptable for the mode, and plain or fancy braids in white and colors are the preferred trimming. Anchors, stars, and other emblems may be embroidered in the corners of the collar, if liked.

This pattern is in five sizes for boys from two to six years of age.

FIGURE NO. 491 K.

1890

LITTLE BOYS' SUIT

3478
Front View.

3478
Back View.

This pattern is in five sizes for boys from two to six years of age. The costume is here shown made of gray-and-blue striped suiting and plain blue serge, figured wash silk being used for the blouse. The skirt is arranged in kilt-plaits that turn toward the back, and is plain at the center of the front, where the ends are widely lapped and closed with buttons and button-holes. The upper edge of the skirt is joined to a sleeveless body. The cap is here shown developed in serge. The crown is formed of six sections that meet at the center beneath a button, and a visor stiffened with canvas joins the crown across the front. Plain, plaid, striped and mixed suitings may be developed in a skirt of this kind, and the jacket may harmonize or contrast with it. Wash silk, percale, cambric, etc., may be employed for the blouse, and the cap may be of velvet, plush or cloth or of material matching the suit.

1890

BOYS' FOUR-BUTTON SACK COAT WITHOUT A SEAM AT THE BACK

Mixed suiting was chosen for the coat in this instance. The back is made without a center seam, and at the side seams, which are curved to gracefully define the form, are formed short vents. All the pockets are finished with flaps that have rounding lower front corners. The sleeves are of stylish width, and a button decorates the back of each wrist. All the edges of the coat are finished with a row of stitching made close to them. Rough, mixed, shot, striped, checked and plaid suitings, and cheviots, tweeds, serges and flannels are stylish for coats of this description, and stitching will form a fashionable edge finish.

This pattern is in thirteen sizes for boys from four to sixteen years of age.

3481
Front View.

3481
Back View.

1890

LITTLE BOYS' DRESS

This stylish little dress is shown made of gray serge, black velvet ribbon and buttons contributing the trimming. It is also shown developed in plaid gingham and decorated with narrow Hamburg embroidered edging.

Dress goods of all varieties will develop satisfactorily by the mode, but cheviot, tweed, flannel, and gingham in checks or plaids are most favored. Braid or stitching may form the finish, and velvet may be employed for the collar, cuffs and belt sections. A pretty development of the mode unites Scotch plaid wool goods and black velvet, with tiny black ball buttons for decoration. The jacket fronts are of velvet, and so are the belt sections and collar; and the wrists are finished with pointed cuff of velvet that are decorated at the back with a cluster of buttons.

Ages two to six years.

3375
Front View.

3375
Back View.

1890

BOYS' SAILOR SUIT

3482
Front View.

3482
Back View.

The pattern is in twelve sizes for boys from four to fifteen years.

Dark-blue flannel was here selected for the suit, and machine-stitching, embroidered emblems and a ribbon bow comprise the decorations. The blouse is made over an under-waist, and is cut out at the neck to accommodate a deep sailor collar and disclose a vest that is attached to the under-waist by buttons and button-holes. The lower edge of the blouse and under-waist are gathered to one band, and the full sleeves are plaited at the bottom and finished with pointed cuffs. The trousers are shaped by the customary seams and flare well over the boot in regulation sailor style. The fronts close with a fly, and the back is adjusted smoothly by hip darts. Pockets are inserted in the leg seams, and a hip pocket is inserted at the right side of the back. Flannel, serge and cloth are generally used for sailor suits, the favorite hues being blue and white, either in solid colors or in stripes. Nautical items may be embroidered on the collar and vest.

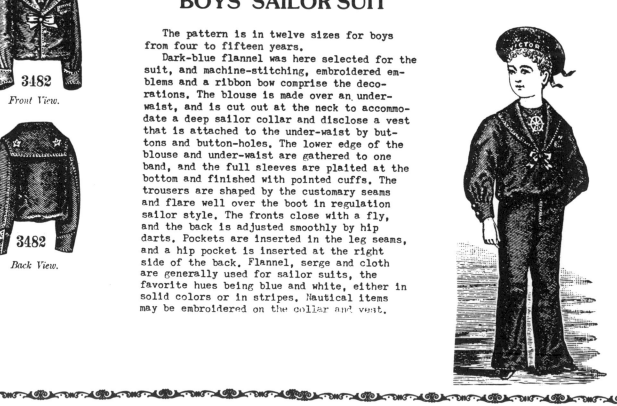

1892

LITTLE BOYS' SUIT

This suit pattern is in seven sizes for little boys from two to eight years.

White flannel and linen lawn are here united in the suit. The trousers extend to the knee and are shaped by the usual seams; they are joined to an under-waist and are closed at the sides with buttonholes and buttons.

The blouse droops in characteristic fashion. The deep, round collar is trimmed with a frill of the material, and between its flaring ends a silk scarf is bowed. Flannel, serge and other materials devoted to suits of this kind will develop nicely; and for summer wear seersucker or Jersey cloth will be stylish and comfortable. The blouse will usually be of lawn, percale or chambray; and the cap may match or contrast with the suit.

The cap is made of white flannel. Six triangular sections are united to form the crown, a peak stiffened with canvas is joined to the front of the crown, and a button ornaments the top.

4459
Front View.

4459
Back View.

1892

LITTLE BOYS' COSTUME

Cheviot, velvet, all-over embroidery and linen lawn are combined in this costume. The skirt is arranged in kilt-plaits all around and is attached to a sleeveless underwaist having only shoulder seams and closed at the front.

The kilt-skirt may be of cheviot, serge, percales or any preferred variety of woolen or cotton goods. The blouse may be of linen lawn, India silk, wash silk, percale or any sheer fabric and frills of lace or embroidery may supply the decoration. Velvet, cloth or pique may be used for the jacket; it may match or contrast with the skirt and braid, buttons or feather-stitching may be added for garniture.

This pattern comes in six sizes for little boys from two to seven years of age.

4460
Front View.

4460
Back View.

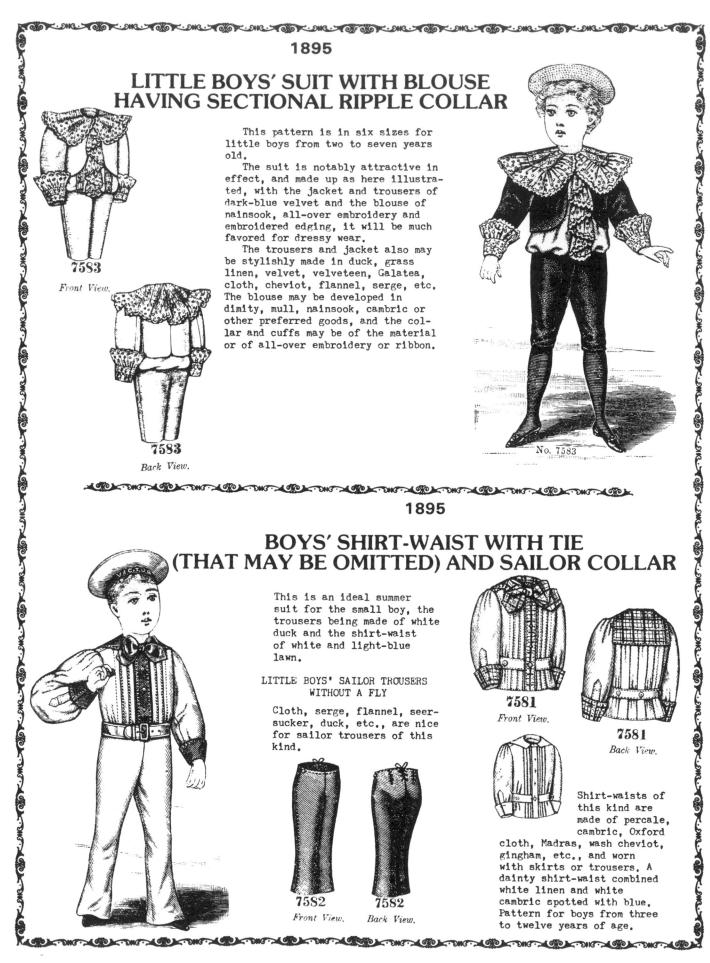

1895

LITTLE BOYS' SUIT WITH BLOUSE HAVING SECTIONAL RIPPLE COLLAR

This pattern is in six sizes for little boys from two to seven years old.

The suit is notably attractive in effect, and made up as here illustrated, with the jacket and trousers of dark-blue velvet and the blouse of nainsook, all-over embroidery and embroidered edging, it will be much favored for dressy wear.

The trousers and jacket also may be stylishly made in duck, grass linen, velvet, velveteen, Galatea, cloth, cheviot, flannel, serge, etc. The blouse may be developed in dimity, mull, nainsook, cambric or other preferred goods, and the collar and cuffs may be of the material or of all-over embroidery or ribbon.

7583
Front View.

7583
Back View.

No. 7583

1895

BOYS' SHIRT-WAIST WITH TIE (THAT MAY BE OMITTED) AND SAILOR COLLAR

This is an ideal summer suit for the small boy, the trousers being made of white duck and the shirt-waist of white and light-blue lawn.

LITTLE BOYS' SAILOR TROUSERS WITHOUT A FLY

Cloth, serge, flannel, seersucker, duck, etc., are nice for sailor trousers of this kind.

7581
Front View.

7581
Back View.

7582
Front View.

7582
Back View.

Shirt-waists of this kind are made of percale, cambric, Oxford cloth, Madras, wash cheviot, gingham, etc., and worn with skirts or trousers. A dainty shirt-waist combined white linen and white cambric spotted with blue. Pattern for boys from three to twelve years of age.

1897

LITTLE BOYS' DRESS

9346
Front View.
LITTLE BOYS' DRESS.

Serge, cashmere and other woolens, as well as gingham, linen and various washable materials, may be made up in this way, with braid, lace or embroidered edging for ornamentation. A dress of Scotch plaid serge may be fashioned after this design with plain serge matching the prevailing color in the plaid for the collar, cuffs and belt. Gilt soutache braid may follow the edges of these accessories. This pattern is in four sizes for little boys from two to five years old.

9346
Back View.
LITTLE BOYS' DRESS.

1897

BOYS' NORFOLK SUIT
Having Knickerbocker Trousers With A Fly
(Known As The Tyrolean Or Chamois Hunter Suit)

Front View.

The suit pattern is in eight sizes for boys from five to twelve years of age.

The Norfolk suit here pictured made of fancy cheviot and finished with machine-stitching and buttons is fashionably known as the Tyrolean or chamois-hunter's suit. The knickerbocker trousers are made with a fly and droop over the knees, where they are drawn in with elastics. The Norfolk jacket consists of a yoke upper portion to which the back and fronts are sewed. A box-plait is applied at the center of the back and similar plaits are arranged on the fronts at each side of the closing. Above the closing the front yokes are reversed in pointed lapels that meet the ends of the rolling coat collar in notches. Large patch pockets are stitched to the fronts back of the plaits, and a belt passed beneath the plaits and under straps stitched over the side seams surrounds the waist. The sleeves are finished at the wrists with stitching and buttons. Scotch tweed and heavy suitings will make up nicely in this suit for cold weather; serge, flannel and light-weight suitings may be selected for the intermediate seasons.

The cap matches the suit. It consists of joined sections that meet in a point at the center under a button. The front of the cap droops over the visor.

9350
Back View.

1898

LITTLE BOYS' MIDDY COSTUME

White and blue serge are here united in this handsome middy costume and the tailor finish is given by machine stitching. The middy vest is closed at the back and finished with a neck-band. The fronts are wide apart all the way and have square lower corners. Cloth in blue, green, gray or brown with a contrasting color for the vest and sailor collar will make very becoming costumes of this style.

Flannel, serge, pique, crash and linen duck may also be chosen. Pattern comes in four sizes for little boys from two to five.

9962
Back View.

9962
Front View.

1898

LITTLE BOYS' SUIT CONSISTING OF A JACKET, A VEST WITH SAILOR COLLAR AND SHIELD, AND SHORT TROUSSERS WITHOUT A FLY (KNOWN AS THE MAN-O'-WAR SUIT)

9944
Front View.

9944
Back View.

LITTLE BOYS' SUIT

This pattern is in seven sizes for little boys from four to ten years of age. This smart suit is known as the Man-o'-War suit, and is here shown in a combination of blue-and-white striped Galatea and white duck, with stitching, buttons and an embroidered emblem on the shield for a finish. The back of the jacket is shaped, and the fronts fall wide apart over a low-cut double-breasted vest having a large sailor-collar, that is worn over the sailor collar of the jacket. A shield completed with a low neck band is buttoned to the vest. The sleeves are of comfortable width. The short trousers are close fitting and are buttoned at the sides.

Suits like this may be suitably made of white duck, with dark-blue duck for the vest collar and shield, and also of flannel in two colors. Braid is sometimes added for a finish.

The hat is a sailor shape in straw.

FIGURE No. 192 G.—This illustrates LITTLE BOYS' SUIT.—The pattern is No. 9944.

LITTLE BOY'S SUIT, CONSISTING OF A JACKET, MIDDY VEST, AND SHORT TROUSERS WITHOUT A FLY.

3110
Front View.

3110
Back View.

Navy-blue cloth was selected for developing this suit, with pique for the vest and black satin for the collar facing, machine-stitching giving a neat finish.

The fronts are shaped low to accommodate a shawl collar that is seamed at the back and has rounding ends.

An embroidered emblem decorates the front of the middy vest, which is joined to the backs in shoulder and underarm seams.

The trousers are shaped with inside and outside leg seams and a center seam and are fitted with hip darts. Side pockets and a right hip-pocket are inserted and the closing is made at the sides.

LITTLE BOY'S SUIT, CONSISTING OF A JACKET, VEST AND SHORT TROUSERS WITHOUT A FLY.

3137
Front View.

3137
Back View.

No. 3137. Blue broadcloth was here used in the development of this attractive suit, with silk for inlaying the lapels of the jacket, and buttons and machine-stitching for a finish. The vest is shaped with the customary seams on the shoulders, under the arms and at the center of the back, and the closing is made with buttons and buttonholes at the front.

The short trousers are shaped with inside and outside leg seams and a center seam and are ornamented with a small bow and buckle tacked at the bottom of each outside seam. They are smooth at the top, fitted with hip darts, and are closed at the sides with buttons and buttonholes.

LITTLE BOY'S RUSSIAN SUIT WITH STOLE OR REGUALR SAILOR-COLLAR.

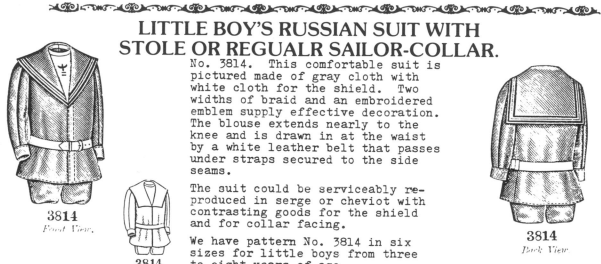

3814
Front View.

3814

3814
Back View.

No. 3814. This comfortable suit is pictured made of gray cloth with white cloth for the shield. Two widths of braid and an embroidered emblem supply effective decoration. The blouse extends nearly to the knee and is drawn in at the waist by a white leather belt that passes under straps secured to the side seams.

The suit could be serviceably reproduced in serge or cheviot with contrasting goods for the shield and for collar facing.

We have pattern No. 3814 in six sizes for little boys from three to eight years of age.

SECTION ONE
Antique Children's Fashions
A Handbook for Doll Costumers

Patterns: Background and History

The intent of this handbook is to provide readers with some expertise in costuming dolls and, therefore, concentrates on practical aspects of creating something that has an old-fashioned look. However, it is interesting to know a little about the development of some of our modern conveniences such as patterns and sewing machines, and to contrast the old, in their often inconvenient and cumbersome forms, to the streamlined versions available to us today. Occasionally this knowledge influences the work we attempt to reproduce in as original a form as possible, giving us an appreciation of the modern developments in machines and supplies for sewing.

For example, we take our hand-sewing needles for granted; yet only in 1867 were hand-sewing needles redesigned to taper at both ends[1] so that pushed halfway through fabric, the largest part of the needle is reached and the taper enables the needle to slide the rest of the way with ease.

Sewing machines, the first invented by Elias Howe in 1846, were apparently seen as a godsend by sewers and tailors everywhere. A mere 20 years after the invention, it was being manufactured by 20 companies in the United States at a combined rate of 200,000 per year. Sales really skyrocketed when Singer offered a "pay-by-the-month" plan, heretofore an unknown technique in merchandising products.[*]

Patterns . . Butterick first came out with full-size paper patterns in 1865, followed by *McCall Magazine* in 1870. A magazine called the *Metropolitan Monthly,* published by Butterick, was supplemented by Butterick in 1872 with the publication of *The Delineator* magazine which continued to be a major fashion and pattern magazine until publication came to an end in 1937.

At first these patterns were plain tissue paper with perforations to mark style lines, numbers to indicate pattern pieces. No instructions were included at first but after the patterns were packed in envelopes a few hints for assembly were included in some detail, one of the first being called the DELTOR.

Any of these were a tremendous improvement over some of the early European patterns which were printed in small scale, pattern pieces intricately overlaid, one upon the other, in an incredible jumble of dotted, dashed and solid lines which almost required an engineering degree to decode. Even then they usually had to be enlarged on graph paper from a scale of 1/8in (0.31cm) to 1in (2.5cm).

So it can be seen that our modern conveniences make our work simple by comparison, although doll costuming aimed at authenticity of styles, fabrics and sewing techniques is still an involved process which only devoted doll collectors have attempted.

It is our hope that the information contained in this handbook will encourage home sewers to work with greater confidence in costuming their own dolls when necessary to make a finished product which fits the doll, adds to the doll's desirability and teaches something about the styles of yesteryear.

We have tried to cover the process from selecting a pattern through selection of fabrics, fitting, methods of construction and use of trim.

Two glossaries include information about terms found relating to costumes of the late 19th century and descriptions of fabrics to which reference is made in fashion books of that period, many of which are no longer available on our modern market and with which many of us are totally unfamiliar.

The emphasis of this book is entirely on children's clothes, about which only a limited body of correlated information is available in a simplified form for home sewers. This area of concentration on girl-child dolls was selected because of the relatively large numbers of child dolls found in doll collections.

In the early days of doll manufacture we know that many dolls were dressed as adults, following the contemporary styles. Indeed, little girls to this day tend to dress their dolls as adults, even though there are often but slight differences in little girls' and ladies' dresses. One of the most striking examples early on and now also is the bridal gown, so dear to the hearts of many little girls.

However, as French bébés and later German bisques came into being, the practice changed and dolls began to appear dressed in miniature costumes copied from children's clothes. Monsieur Jumeau made an effort to dress his dolls as little girls and subsequently earned many medals for his efforts in this direction, as in 1876 in the Philadelphia Exposition.[2]

We have, therefore, elected to represent doll costumes of the period from 1877 to 1900, using as an authority for the styles shown in this handbook the early *The Delineator* magazines of the period mentioned. We have in fact used *only The Delineators* from 1877 onward and wherever possible in our patterns show a reprint of the original text. For the fashion pages shown in this book it was not practicable to use the whole text given with each pattern so we have, instead, used lines from the texts showing sizes for which each pattern was available, fabrics used, and colors popular at the time. This should serve as a convenient reference when there is doubt about the age at which a particular style was used (viz. a boy of five years in kilts or other forms of dress) or the sizes included in certain designated ages different from our concept of that term (i.e. children . . . three to twelve years).

Consulting these fashion plates, one may also see a slow progression of styles over the period of some 20 years, and can verify the use of certain colors which now seem alien to children's clothes. Children were not always dressed in fluffy pinks and blues but frequently in somber dark colors such as maroon and navy blue.

For antique dolls it is preferable always to use fabrics which were available at the time of the doll's manufacture.

[1]Arnold, Janet, *Patterns of Fashion,* Wace & Company, Ltd, 1966, p. 3.

[*]Brandon, Ruth. A Capitalist Romance . . . Singer and the Sewing Machine. J. B. Limincott Company, New York 1977.

[2]Coleman, Elizabeth, *Dolls, Makers and Marks,* Washington, D. C., 1966.

ALLOWANCES when fitting doll clothes (or) HOW MUCH IS ENOUGH .. or TOO much.

Consider the doll - - she toils not, nor does she spin. Therefore, the garments need no allowances for shoulder movements, or bending over, or reaching upward. On the other hand, neither does the doll want to be a victim of "gap-osis," or of unpleasant fabric stretch marks across chest and shoulders, wrinkles under the arms, or a general appearance of bagginess when a neat fit is desirable. So try to keep in mind, when fitting a basic muslin pattern (and, as we repeat endlessly, over ALL underwear planned for the costume) that:

1. CLOSURES: They should come together smoothly and neatly with no pull on buttons or hooks and eyes. There should be a sufficient number of buttons (or whatever) to provide complete closing (as for example at 1in [2.5cm] to 1½in [3.8cm] intervals). A good practice is to complete closure (front, back or side front) with buttons or whatever is used, *before* fitting side seams, or depending on dress style, the center back seam, as further insurance of good fit.

2. SLEEVES:

    a. This is repetitive, but coat or fitted sleeves hang straight from the shoulder line, with no gathers or tucks around the armseye, should fit snugly without pulling around upper arms, and taper to a size which allows the sleeve to slide over the doll's hand. Alternately a 1in (2.5cm) or 1½in (3.8cm) opening slit may be made at the wrist and closed with hook and threaded loop, allowing for a closer fit around the wrist.

    b. It should be noted that coat or tailored sleeves are usually made in two parts with the seams approximately midway between top and bottom of armseye, back and front. In very small sizes, for ease in construction the sleeve may be made with only ONE seam. This seam will NOT be at underarm, but in the back midway between top and bottom of armseye.

3. BODY OF DRESS: In some styles easing is not so important, but in a princess style or fitted A-line at the underarm and across the chest there should be just enough allowance to permit a smooth fit without any pull across front or back. No "moving" allowance is necessary as in the case of ladies' clothes.

4. BODICE: Here a more tightly fitted garment is desirable . . *snug* might describe it, and the method of alternating hooks and eyes on each side of closure as described in *Illustration 117* will prevent gaping and pulling. The length of the bodice should be carefully noted, and darts generously used for a tightly fitted waist to help prevent the bodice from sliding upward and wrinkling.

5. NECKLINE: The neck of a dress, if high, should fit snugly around the neck where the socket head touches the torso. When fitting a low neckline around a shoulder plate, it is essential to fit neckline in such a way that it lies flat and close to the shoulder plate. The method described under fitting necklines, of using a double thread to make a fine gathering stitch around the neck of the dress, pulling in gently to a perfect fit, is also applicable here, and serves the double purpose of preventing stretching as the facing is applied.

6. SHOULDER LINE: In most old dresses it may be noted that the shoulder seam is not at the highest point of the shoulder, but a full seam allowance toward the back. Our patterns are made with this feature in mind, so it is necessary to remember this when fitting shoulder seams.

7. HEMLINE: Dolls are generally well-behaved when dresses are being fitted, but do tend to be fractious when it comes to hemming. Before setting the hemline, check to be sure that the doll has not slumped in the stand, or that the stem has not lowered allowing the doll's legs to buckle. Also, dolls sometimes tend to slide backward or forward in the stand. After all these possibilities have been checked, proceed to measure from the floor (table) around the hemline.

The length of a dress depends on the style of dress, the period (Kate Greenaway models revived for a few years in the early 1890s were almost floor length, and some child dolls of the 1870s to 1880s appear in very short dresses, if we can judge by the appearance of some of the "all-original" dolls shown).

Generally speaking, a doll dress hemline may come just below the knee, or even a little shorter, again depending on the period of the costume.

SECTION TWO
How To Make A Basic Doll Pattern

Doll pattern designers make every effort to produce a pattern which can be used for a doll with a minimum of fitting. However, doll bodies are like "people" bodies - - tall and slender, short and plump, broad or narrow shouldered, and so forth. Therefore, to achieve a well-fitted costume, it is necessary to make a basic pattern first, correcting obvious problems in the areas mentioned. This is actually less tedious than first appears, as no fine sewing or finishing is required and the process is less devastating than to agonize over a poorly fitted dress or the waste of beautiful material after it is too late to make vital alterations.

Again we should like to stress a point already made, that underwear for a doll must be completed, put on the doll, and the doll placed on a stand before starting the basic pattern. You may note that we mention putting the doll on a stand. Unfortunately the waist stem of a stand takes space around which a fitted dress will not fit properly unless allowance is made in the initial fitting.* So dress the doll in her chemise, drawers, and petticoat or slip and you are ready to start altering the pattern to fit the doll to be dressed.

CUTTING DETAILS FOR A BASIC PATTERN:

a. Cut front, back and sleeves of unbleached muslin, noting any darts or fitting lines. Using large machine-basting stitch, sew side seams, shoulder seams (and for princess style, side front and side back seams). Machine-baste around neckline on seam line, checking to be sure that seam allowance on pattern is used. Fold along fold lines for closure, either front or back. Fit on doll, remembering instructions previously given to put on all underwear doll is to be wearing, and fit over the doll on the stand. Pin closure with 1/2in (1.3cm) overlap.

Now you are ready to examine the following areas in which correct fitting is important, and to make alterations as noted.

SHOULDER:

b. Check shoulder seams: too wide? Take a pencil and mark new seam line at opening between shoulder and upper arm. Too narrow? Glue or baste on a small piece of fabric where needed and mark a new seam line.

SEAM LINE:

c. Check side seam: too much material? Pin out excess and mark a new seam line. Too small? First remove stitching, then add (glue or baste on) a small strip of fabric to both side seams, front and back. Pin to correct size and use pencil to mark new stitching line. If working with a princess style you might find it necessary to add fabric to the front and/or back seams, or if the dress is too large, pin out excess fabric at seams. Again, whatever changes are made should be marked clearly since these will be the basis for altering the pattern.

*See Section Three on STANDS for ways of altering stands to fit individual dolls.

NECKLINE:

d. Check neckline. Note the *staystitching* which you sewed along the seam line. First clip at 1/2in (1.3cm) intervals through the seam allowance to the staystitching. If the neckline is too tight, clip through stitching further to relieve tension, providing the difference is NOT greater than 1/8in (0.31cm). If the difference is greater, slit pattern down center front and add a piece of fabric which allows for correct fitting. Glue or baste this piece of fabric to show the correction. It might be necessary to add a little at the neckline for a full 1/4in (0.65cm) seam allowance. Keep in mind that the neckline should fit snugly around doll's neck, lying flat across the front and around shoulders, presuming that the pattern is styled to form a high neckline. If the neckline is scooped out, as with a boat neckline, fit carefully around shoulder plate so that the neckline will stay in place with no gaps or slipping.

NECKLINE PATTERN:

It is sometimes difficult to achieve the goal of a perfectly fitted neckline even with the above information. Another method is to cut a cardboard to fit the neckline and use this to alter the pattern. To do this refer to *Illustration 2* and follow directions given with the illustration.

HEM:

e. Hemline: Too long? Cut off excess but allow *at least* 2in (5.1cm) for hem. If this later appears to be more than you need, it can be further shortened. Too short? Add on a piece of fabric (again, glue or baste) making sure of enough fabric for a 2in (5.1cm) hem. It is also a good idea to "hang" the dress as one does an adult dress, by using a ruler to mark the correct number of inches from the floor (table) to hemline, and mark with pencil or pins. Straighten hemline, and again check so that you will have a 2in (5.1cm) hem allowance after trimming off the excess.

SLEEVE:

f. Sleeve: Machine-baste sleeve seam or seams. Run two rows of gathering threads along cap of sleeve between notches, one each side of the seam line. Pull gently to form a small cap. See *Illustrations 3 and 4.* Matching notches if there are any shown, or other sewing guides, pin in place and baste. Is sleeve long enough? Fine!

(1) If it is short, again add a piece of fabric to correct length plus 1/2in (1.3cm) turn for hem.

(2) Does sleeve fit around arm just right, or is it too loose, presuming you are fitting a tailored (coat) sleeve? If so, pin out excess along seam or seams, and mark new stitching line with a pencil.

(3) Does sleeve hang straight from shoulder without wrinkling or pulling? If either of these faults exist, try adjusting by sliding sleeve a little to right or left in the armseye and re-pin. It might be necessary to narrow the seam allowance of sleeve at shoulder to allow a little more fullness. When adjustment satisfies you, pencil in corrections for use later on.

CORRECTED PATTERN:

g. Making sure that all corrections have been marked with pencil along new stitching lines, take dress off doll, remove ALL stitching and all pins, and press. Take each piece of the basic pattern separately, transfer adjustments to tissue pattern, and re-adjust seam allowances or add where necessary so that you have a 1/4in (0.65cm) seam allowance all around the pattern (OR WHATEVER SEAM ALLOWANCE IS REQUIRED ON THE PATTERN YOU ARE USING).

Refer to *Illustration 5* which shows these areas in which adjustments may have to be made.

CUTTING DRESS AND LINING FROM BASIC PATTERN:

h. Now with your newly adjusted pattern, cut dress lining and dress, following procedure outlined in the pattern you are using, or use HINT regarding cutting on Pages 113 and 114.

While this may seem a somewhat tedious process, it is nevertheless worth the fine results achieved . . a dress with neatly fitting neckline and sleeves, a waistline correctly placed, and hemline even. It is, in fact, just this process which is followed by fine costumers who work on a contract basis and who take pride in their fine workmanship.

CARDBOARD NECK PATTERN

To fit doll's neck perfectly, follow directions below.

1. Cut two half-circles of cardboard, and carefully trim on the inside until the two pieces meet and fit doll's neck perfectly. Pin shoulders of pattern together on *seam* line. Lay cardboard circle over pattern to determine alterations to be made on pattern to fit doll's neck perfectly. Neckline may be oval rather than round so adjust accordingly.

Illustrations 3 and 4. Fitting a sleeve.

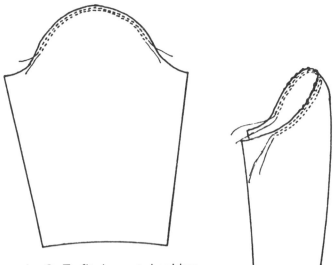

Illustration 3. To fit sleeve at shoulder:
1. Place two rows of gathering stitches shown, 1/8in (0.31cm) apart.
2. Pull gently to form small cap.

Illustration 4. Sleeve cap showing cupping.

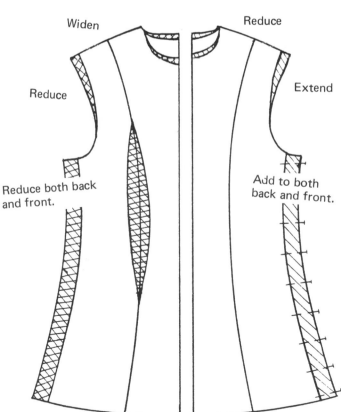

Illustration 5. Basic dress with fitting notes.

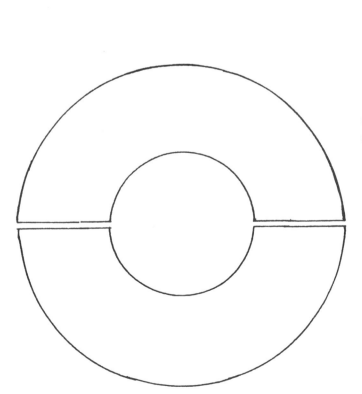

Illustration 2. Cardboard pattern for fitting neckline.

SECTION THREE
Stands
How to Adapt Stands to Problem Dolls

At best a doll stand provides a secure framework so that a doll can be shown standing up, allowing size and details of costumes to be more apparent and visible. Stands also protect dolls from wear and tear on joints (particularly on ball-jointed bodies) where a sitting position puts strain on the elastic and the sockets.

At their worst, stands can be stubborn, unbending pieces of wire that allow the doll to slip, to lean forward or backward, or to slip off at the waist ring. Some of the following may help you to solve these problems. This information is included in costuming because it is felt that having a doll secured on an adequate stand is essential to the fitting process.

First, keep in mind that the usual metal stands now in use consist of a base with a stem into which fits a looped wire forming a ring at the top which more or less fits a doll's waist. This adds bulk to a doll's waist, and must be taken into account when fitting garments on the doll. Our patterns are designed to fit OVER the metal ring.

The following pages include an illustration of a standard stand with all of the parts labeled so that you will be able to refer to the labels as you find them used in the ten suggestions for altering stands to fit your dolls. *Illustration 6.*

The last adaptation is a really fine one designed for use with kid bodies and for many chinas (porcelains) that tend to be top-heavy. This is offered through the courtesy of Helen Barglebaugh and May Wenzel who printed it in a 1979 issue of their *Doll Quarterly*. (See Bibliography.)

The 13 adaptations of the stand, including ten illustrations, 7 through 16, follow:

1. If the waist circle fits fairly well but you worry about the doll slipping, slide strong cord or twill tape through the eyelets on the circle of wire and tie cord securely after doll has been positioned correctly on the stand, and after doll has been dressed in drawers and chemise.

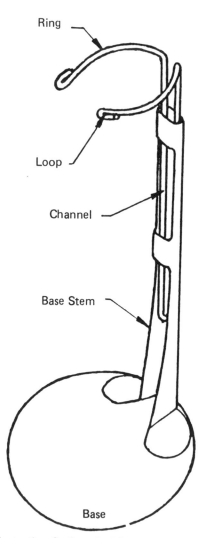

Ring

Loop

Channel

Base Stem

Base

Illustration 6. Stand with parts labeled.

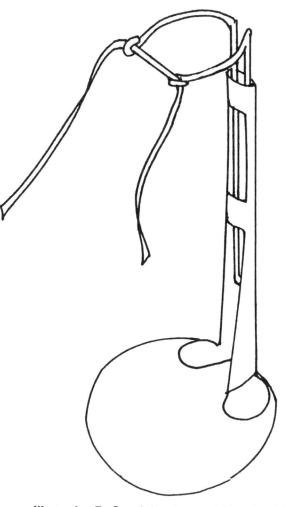

Illustration 7. Stand showing cord for tying doll.

2. For dolls with large "bottoms" which hit the stem and prevent the doll from standing upright, use pliers and vise to bend the WIRE STEM forward 1in (2.5cm) or more below the waist ring. This should allow the bottom of the torso to swing free from the stand and doll to remain upright.

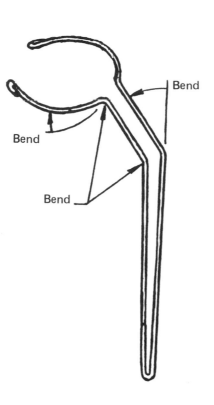

Illustration 8. Stand showing ring stem bent forward.

3. Sometimes a doll will stand in a better position if the metal stem is bent forward slightly. Experiment to determine the exact angle best for a particular doll.

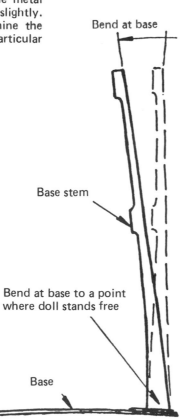

Bend at base

Base stem

Bend at base to a point where doll stands free

Base

Illustration 9. Stand showing stem bent forward.

4. Particularly for cloth-bodied dolls: Cut off the eyelet from 1/2in (1.3cm) to 1in (2.5cm) back from the ends of the circle. Using white glue and thin cotton fabric (or tape) about 1/4in (0.45cm) to 1/2in (1.3cm) wide wrap the wire ends as shown, allowing about 6in (15.2cm) of the fabric or tape at each end for ties. With underwear on doll, place doll on stand positioned correctly, and tie securely.

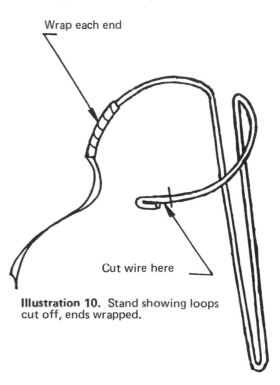

Wrap each end

Cut wire here

Illustration 10. Stand showing loops cut off, ends wrapped.

5. If the wire ring does not conform to doll's waistline, bulging out because of the contour of the circle, the circle is too round and needs to be straightened out. Experiment with pliers and vise to reduce the degree of "roundness" until it fits doll's waist. For heavy stands this takes strength. (We have learned to put the wire ring on the floor, stepping on it at the eyelet end, and then exerting pressure to straighten out the curve.)

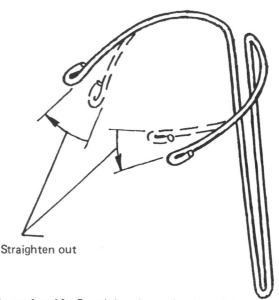

Straighten out

Illustration 11. Stand showing reshaping of ring.

71

6. **SADDLE STAND.** This type of modification will provide a stand which will not use the heavy metal ring around the doll's waist, which interferes with proper fit of tight bodices such as those often made for French Fashions. The metal ring of an ordinary stand has been redesigned (using vise and pliers) to fit the doll as one rides a saddle, thus the name. It is best to experiment with a small-sized stand and relatively lightweight wire to get an idea of the shaping required. This stand is practical only when a doll has a rather stiff torso which does not allow any bending at waist or leg joints. This stand fits between doll's legs. The metal ring and stem are *reversed,* back to front, when placed in the channel of the base.

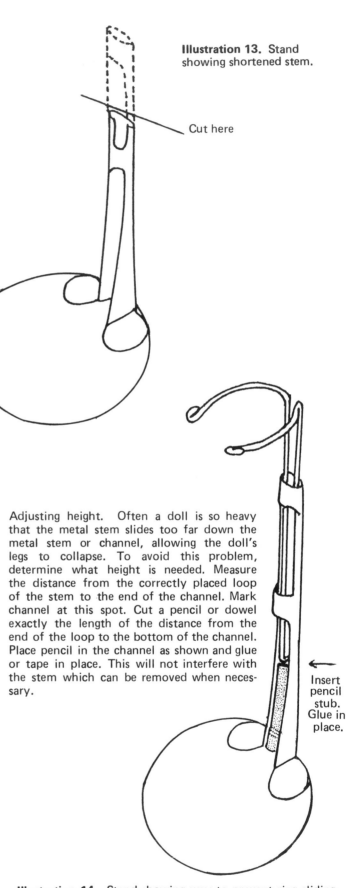

Illustration 13. Stand showing shortened stem.

Cut here

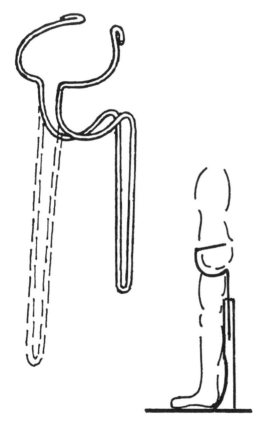

Illustration 12. Stand showing "saddle" adjustment.

8. Adjusting height. Often a doll is so heavy that the metal stem slides too far down the metal stem or channel, allowing the doll's legs to collapse. To avoid this problem, determine what height is needed. Measure the distance from the correctly placed loop of the stem to the end of the channel. Mark channel at this spot. Cut a pencil or dowel exactly the length of the distance from the end of the loop to the bottom of the channel. Place pencil in the channel as shown and glue or tape in place. This will not interfere with the stem which can be removed when necessary.

Insert pencil stub. Glue in place.

7. **ELIMINATE "DANGLE."** There is a problem doll from 8in (20.3cm) to 12in (30.5cm) which is too short for a stand that has a base large enough to hold the doll securely without danger of tipping, but is much too large for the size stand intended for dolls that height. The base cannot be widened as is suggested here in some cases because the metal ring would then be much too small for this type of doll. Solution: Use a number 2500 (number 2) stand, but shorten the stem from 1in (2.5cm) to 2in (5.1cm). After cutting at the point which you have decided is satisfactory for your doll, with pliers restore the original curve to the top of the stem or channel. In most cases it will be necessary to bend the metal stem forward to some degree as described in *Illustration 9,* or you may be able to use a waist ring from the next smaller stand available.

Illustration 14. Stand showing way to prevent ring sliding in channel.

9. If a doll's balance seems precarious because the circular base is too small (this often happens with very tall dolls that have slender waists) cut a circle of thin plywood or masonite (for lightweight stands heavy cardboard would suffice) about 2in (5.1cm) or 3in (7.6cm) larger in diameter than the circular base. Glue this to the underpart of the circular base. This will add security and balance to the stand. The whole base may be covered with felt to hide the added support.

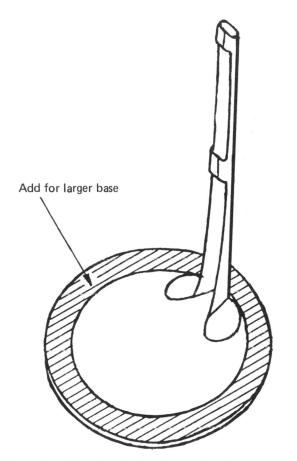

Add for larger base

Illustration 15. Stand showing widened base to prevent tipping.

10. If your doll slips because the metal base is smooth, cut a circle of velvet, felt, or some other attractive fabric the size of the circular base, clip at one point to allow for the stem. Glue this to the top of the base. This adds enough friction to keep the doll's feet from sliding forward.
11. To protect table tops add a piece of felt to the underside of the circular base, gluing it in place.
12. To protect the doll body from the metal ring, slide large plastic straws over each end. For the larger stand you might have to cut off the large loop which, in any case, ruins the lines of a close-fitting dress.
13. CORSET/DOLL STAND HARNESS. (Reprinted here courtesy of Helen Barglebaugh and May Wenzel who edit *Costume Quarterly For Doll Collectors*.)
   This stand was designed to hold a fashion doll securely in place without unsightly ridges at the waist, formed by the ring of a standard metal stand.

"STAND: Modify an ordinary metal doll stand by removing metal stem and substituting a 3/32in (0.23cm) x 1/2in (1.3cm) aluminum strip cut to fit the stand channel from its base to upper back of doll.

"Pry stand locking bars apart to fit strip into channel and firmly close again over the strip with pliers. Round and smooth top of strip with a file before bending it to match doll center back contours. Upper part of strip fits into a harness casing." (This harness is in the form of a corset so it serves the double purpose of holding the doll up, and of providing one undergarment.)

"Corset-harness: Shape shown below is only suggested. *Illustration 16.* Each doll must be fitted individually. Prepare a pattern by measuring center back below shoulderplate to wasitline. Cut bias muslin as wide as that measurement. Wrap doll above waist in bias-cut muslin; stretch to eliminate side creases. Pull tight and pin at center front. Mark center front and center back, upper and lower edges of a final harness.

"Unpin and trim muslin to marks. Add 1/2in (1.3cm) to each center front straight edge for facings. Use muslin pattern to cut corset-harness in cotton sateen backed with strong jean fabric. Keep fabric straight grain aligned with center back. Mark pattern on right side of sateen, baste sateen over jean fabric, and cut. Fold 1/2in (1.3cm) of each center front to inside as facing. Snip basting at lower center back and slip doubled glove leather between sateen and jean fabric as casing reinforcement. Sew two rows of stitching around stand casing at center fronts. Sew 1/4in (0.65cm) from upper and lower raw edges (except in area of casing opening).

"Trim raw edges with pinking or scalloping shears. Narrow lace can also be used along edges. Small brass eyelets complete front of corset/doll stand harness.

"Lace [the] harness firmly on doll. Fit upper part of aluminum strip into harness casing and adjust as necessary. Keep feet slightly above stand base. Space will eventually be taken by shoe innersole and soles . . . .

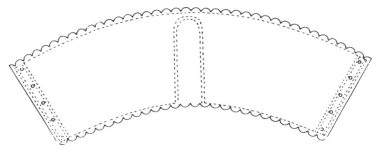

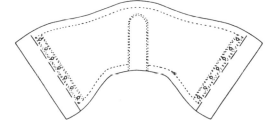

Illustration 16. Two views of corset shapes.

OUR NOTE: See Stand number 3 for information about tilting channel base stem forward slightly to let doll stand clear.

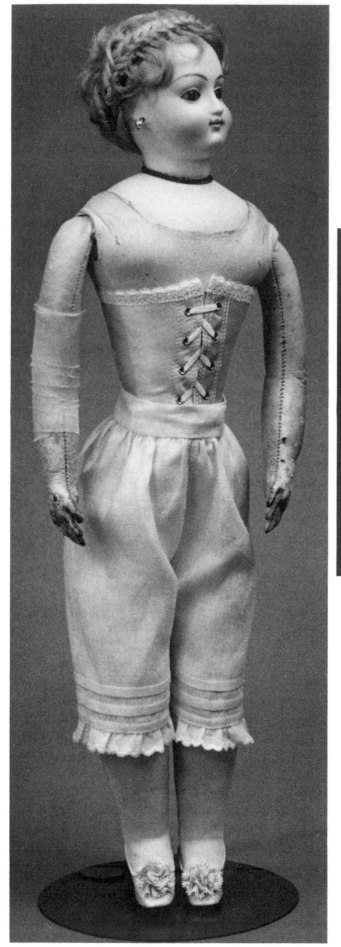

MORE HELP TO ASSIST IN EASING DOLL ONTO STAND:

"Fasten corset/harness on doll. Slip doll, feet first, through chemise neck opening. Ease arms into sleeves, while chemise is at hip-level. Have the stockings in place before drawers are lifted over feet. Feed aluminum stand strip into harness back casing. The drawers rest under back strip at waistline, and chemise over it . . . .

"Unfortunately some fashion lady dolls have such a pronounced posterior that the bent-to-shape aluminum strip will not feed into back casing after harness is laced. To overcome this fault place corset/harness in position on metal stand before dressing doll in chemise, then firmly lace harness (already on stand) to doll under the chemise."

Illustration 17. Corset-Harness Stand.
Costume Quarterly for Doll Collectors © 1979 May Wenzel and Helen Barglebaugh.

74

SECTION FOUR
Adapting An Old Christening Dress For Doll Garment

Often an old christening dress has beautiful embroidery and handsewn lace. While we do not suggest cutting up a beautiful old dress in excellent condition, it may be possible to salvage some parts of an old dress by using it for a doll. Select a pattern somewhat like that of the original dress, as, for example, a simple yoke dress.

To prepare the dress for cutting, remove sleeves and cut along the seamlines, and press flat. Cut through shoulder seams and open down back (or front if there is a front opening). Cut yoke at least 1in (2.5cm) below the bottom seam to preserve any trim which might be useful for the garment to be made. Press the dress flat.

Using *Illustration 18* for cutting, keep in mind the following points in your planning.

1. Trim should be appropriate in scale for a doll garment . . . tiny tucks, fine lace and correct placement of trim on the doll dress. Heavy hand-crocheted lace is almost always too bulky for a doll garment. Trimming used on a doll dress should be in proportion to the size of the dress. The band of trim on an infant's christening dress may be 12in (30.5cm) wide, much too wide for a 16in (40.6cm) doll. We have, for example, seen drawers cut from a section of an old garment in such a way as to have large tucks from the waistband to the bottom of

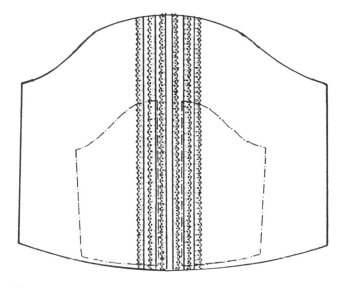

Illustration 19. Christening garment showing sleeve layout.

Too wide for scale of doll dress. Cut as shown and seam down center front and center back.

—————————————————————·— Cutting line.

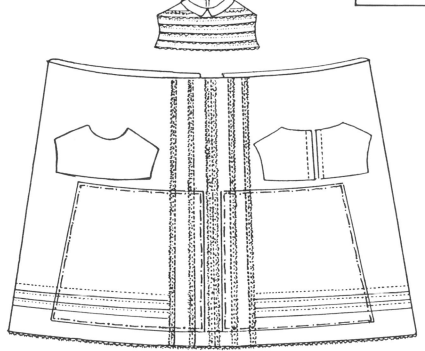

Illustration 18. Christening garment showing pattern layout.

Too wide for scale of doll dress. Cut as shown and seam down center front and center back.

—·———·———·———·———·— Cutting line.

the drawers, an effect quite out of keeping with reasonably proportioned trim.

2. Fit pattern over trim in such a way that it will fall on the correct section of the dress (i.e. with tucks near hemline, but ALLOW for hem). If midsection trim is very wide, it should be narrowed to an acceptable width. Be sure that front and back of dress match. This will show at side seams, but can be controlled easily by marking pattern at point where trim meets at sides.

3. If yoke does not seem right for the pattern, try a section of upper dress and add your own trim. Sometimes it is possible to rip carefully the upper dress and save bits of lace and trim which can be used on a yoke design of your own.

4. Sleeves: Cut as shown in *Illustration 19*. Use bottom trim or part of it if possible, but it is more likely that you will cut the sleeve separately and add trim.

SECTION FIVE
Adapting An Old Petticoat To Doll Underwear:

If you are fortunate enough to have a lady's petticoat with beautiful tucks, you can use it to make doll underwear. Keep in mind always that this is only practical if trim is appropriate in scale for a doll garment . . . tiny tucks, narrow lace and so forth. Do not hesitate to use only part of the trim so that the doll garment will not be laden with heavy lace and broad tucks.

1. Open up one seam of petticoat and cut off band so that the fabric will lie flat. Press.
2. Look at the pattern and visualize where you want tucks and trim on the doll garments. Again, keep in mind that tucks do not go all the way from the waistband to hemline. At most they should cover only the bottom third of the garment. Tucks on drawers should be confined to the area well below the crotch, and the petticoat can be made to correspond.

   Illustration 20 should be of some help in placement of the pattern on an old garment to take full advantage of the attractive tucks and trim without spoiling the simple correct lines of the finished doll garment.

3. Note that almost always the bottom ruffle of an adult garment is too wide for a doll garment. Cut off the ruffle at the gathering line. Press, and re-cut at the correct width for doll garment. Of course, you are wasting some of the skirt, but it is better to waste this part of the ruffle than to ruin the garment you are making.
4. The illustration shows a chemise cut on the fold. If this is not possible, it may be cut crosswise, piecing down center back and opening down center front.

   It can be seen from the illustration that a matching set of chemise, drawers, and petticoat can be made, taking full advantage of the same fabric for each piece. Note that cotton lace can be dyed (see HINTS for help with the dyeing process) to blend perfectly with the possibly yellowed color of the old petticoat. We do not recommend use of bleach in laundering both because it destroys the "old look" of the garment, and because in some cases will cause deterioration of the fabric.

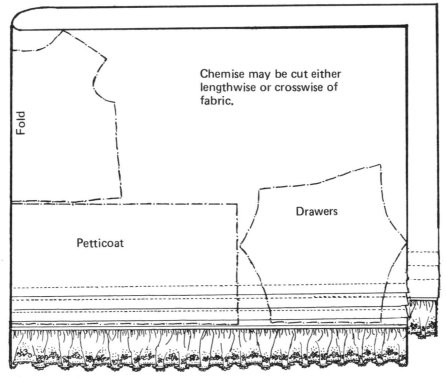

Chemise may be cut either lengthwise or crosswise of fabric.

Fold

Petticoat

Drawers

Shorten and gather.

Illustration 20. Antique petticoat with underwear pattern overlaid.

Usually the border is too wide for doll clothes. Use tucks. Cut border off and narrow to scale.

Shorten and gather bottom ruffle before using. On drawers or petticoat for an 18in (45.7cm) doll, ruffle should not exceed 1½in (3.8cm).

SECTION SIX
A Bit About The History Of Undergarments

DRAWERS:

Ladies' and girls' drawers went through many style changes throughout the years from 1840 to 1920, but not until the pre-1920s do we find the word "panties" creeping into descriptions of doll clothes, and particularly for girls and children.

As drawers, however, they appeared frequently with drawstring tops, sometimes with simple waistbands, closed with buttons and buttonholes, or tied with narrow tape, either at the side or in back. Also found is a blending of the two, a plain band across the front of the drawers from side seam to side seam. From the side seams to center back a small casing was found, from 1/8in (0.31cm) to 1/4in (0.65cm), to accommodate a drawstring. This is an especially practical way to make drawers as they provide a smooth finish across the front and fit a variety of waistlines. In addition, hooks and eyes are found on old garments as far back as the 16th century. Made to hang just below the knees, drawers were usually decorated with three to five tiny tucks and lace gathered or applied without fullness around the bottom edge. As changes gradually occurred, these changes included wider and wider legs, and legs sometimes gathered at the knees with a narrow band to which a ruffle of eyelet embroidery was added.

Combinations of drawers with a chemise top attached (or "combination") appeared in *The Delineator* as early as 1880, both for children and adults, and in the early 1900s, underwear appeared made of knit cotton, called "union suits."

CHEMISES:

Chemises were standard equipment for dolls very early in their manufacture, often being the only garment other than drawers that comprised the costume. Note that we are talking of child dolls, exclusive of fashion dolls which, of course, often had elaborate undergarments including corsets, corset covers and so on.

From chemises developed several related garments, usually taking advantage of this basic garment with adaptations to make it more useful.

In early instances drawers were added to form a chemise-drawers, later called a "combination." A *chemisette* was developed in the form of a dickey or neckpiece to be worn under low-necked dresses. In a way they were even forerunners of the "corset cover," a loose chemise tied down low on the neckline, and extending only a little below the waist. However, we are interested here primarily in chemises for dolls.

Chemises for dolls were generally very simple, usually about mid-thigh length, sometimes with short sleeves and sometimes with no sleeves. The garment could have simple lace trim, a drawstring neckline, and might be opened for only a short distance down the front, or have an opening at the shoulder.

It is tempting when costuming dolls to make chemises with elaborate lace trim around sleeves and neckline but we have discontinued this practice because, especially on small dolls, it adds bulk under dresses, making fitting more difficult.

Tucks are seldom found on chemises but a row of lace added without fullness at the hemline will enhance the appearance of the garment.

PETTICOATS:

Numerous petticoats were worn during this period, both because the dresses were often full and required the bouffant look achieved with several petticoats, and often because before the days of central heating houses were cold, and petticoats served the useful purpose of keeping people warm. Hence, the use of flannel petticoats, some of which were bright red .. although the color probably had nothing to do with "heating" qualities.

Petticoats could be simple, or just as elaborate as the wearer could afford. Late in the century children's petticoats were made with attached tops, and often followed the contour of the dress, so the fullness could be concentrated in the area of a bustle or back fullness.

Old petticoats have been found with both side and back closures, buttoned on both sides, or in the back. Later front bands were replaced by decorative girdles, with drawstrings running from side seams to center back.

Petticoats can be made very simply by following these instructions, using the chart for measurements from sizes 6in (15.2cm) to 24in (61.0cm) in even sizes. For variations of trim consult Fashion Plate, Page 47 for illustrations of petticoats with much variety in the trim used.

YARDAGE CHART FOR DOLL PETTICOATS	
Size of doll	Cut rectangle
6in (15.2cm) doll	2½in (6.4cm) x 10in (25.4cm)
8in (20.3cm) doll	3¼in (8.3cm) x 15in (38.1cm)
10in (25.4cm) doll	4in (10.2cm) x 18in (45.7cm)
12in (30.5cm) doll	5in (12.7cm) x 20in (50.8cm)
14in (35.6cm) doll	6in (15.2cm) x 30in (76.2cm)
16in (40.6cm) doll	7in (17.8cm) x 36in (91.4cm)
18in (45.7cm) doll	8in (20.3cm) x 40in (101.6cm)
20in (50.8cm) doll	9in (22.9cm) x 44in (111.7cm)
22in (55.9cm) doll	11in (27.9cm) x 50in (127.0cm)
24in (61.0cm) doll	13in (33.0cm) x 56in (142.2cm)

APPROXIMATE MEASUREMENTS, for use with knee length dress. Add 1in (2.5cm) if using three tucks. For band, cut fabric 1in (2.5cm) longer than doll's waist measure, and 1in (2.5cm) or 1¼in (3.2cm) wide, using 1/4in (0.65cm) seam allowance.

Illustration 21.

INSTRUCTIONS FOR PETTICOAT:

Sizes given are general and may need to be altered slightly depending on the size of the doll, the kind of dress under which the petticoat is to be worn (if dress is not very full, petticoat should be adjusted accordingly). Also smaller size petticoats will obviously need narrower bands.

An optional choice for something other than a band would be the use of a drawstring. Instead of gathering top of petticoat to a band, turn twice at the top to form a 1/4in (0.65cm) casing and sew securely by machine. Run drawstring through casing. This is particularly useful when you are working with small dolls, or for a doll whose waistline you do not know.

In general 1in (2.5cm) additional length is suggested if tucks are to be used. In larger sizes these measurements allow for a 1½in (3.8cm) hem, but for smaller sizes this hem would be too deep.

INSTRUCTIONS FOR PETTICOATS:
1. Cut a rectangle of cotton the size indicated on the chart for your doll, remembering to add to this length 1in (2.5cm) if you intend to use tucks.
2. Cut a band approximately 1in (2.5cm) longer than the waist measurement of the doll, and about 1in (2.5cm) or 1¼in (3.2cm) wide.
3. Mark tucks as shown on tuck gauge or following instructions under section on tucking.
4. Sew tucks.
5. Turn up hem and apply narrow lace if desired. (See *Illustration 29* for suggestions about applying lace.)
6. Sew narrow ends of rectangle leaving 3in (7.6cm) opening for placket. Hem placket closure by hand.
7. Sew two rows of gathering stitches by hand or by machine at waistline; pull in to fit waistband. Sew on hook and eye, or use buttonhole and button. Short lengths of tape set back about 1in (2.5cm) to 2in (5.1cm) on one side of the band, at the end of the band on the other side of the petticoat allow for considerable adjustment in size.

Illustration 22. Tape closure for petticoat.

DUST RUFFLE:

A dust ruffle was a piece of tarlatan, sometimes with a lace edge, formed in pleats and used as stiffening under children's dresses or under the hems of ladies' skirts. In children's clothes they were suitable only with dropped waistline dresses. They were stitched to the dress where the skirt is joined to the bodice. In ladies' dresses they were used only with floor length garments, which gives a hint about the reason for the name, "dust ruffle."

To make a dust ruffle for a 10in (25.4cm) doll, cut a piece of tarlatan or organdy about 2yd (1.82cm) long and 4in (10.2cm) wide. Fold in half lengthwise and add narrow lace on the folded edge. Pleat all around in desired size pleats (they may be quite large, as for example 1in [2.5cm] pleats) and machine-stitch at the top. If desired, bind top with a strip of lightweight cotton. Tack loosely onto dress lining, the bottom edge of the dust ruffle even with the bottom of dress hem.

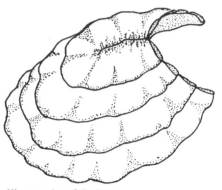

Illustration 25. Bustle. View of bustle with four ruffles.

UNDERWEAR BUSTLE: worn over chemise, drawers and petticoat. (Sizes shown in pattern *Illustration 24* include even sizes from 12in [30.5cm] to 22in [55.9cm]).

INSTRUCTIONS FOR BUSTLE:
1. Cut two pieces of heavy muslin according to pattern.
2. Seam along curved outside edge, clip and turn right sides out. Press.
3. Cut as many pieces of bias muslin as are required for the size you are making, of correct width.* Fold raw edges together and sew with long machine-stitch for gathering, about 1/4in (0.65cm) from raw edges.
   1st Row: Place the longest piece of bias 1/8in (0.31cm) from curved edge of muslin base, gather to fit, and sew in place by machine. Raw edges will be covered by the next ruffle.
   2nd Row: Treat the next longest piece the same way and sew to bustle, laying raw edges of second ruffle about 1/4in (0.65cm) or 3/8in (0.9cm) from edge of base. You should NOT stitch through first ruffle.
   3rd and 4th Rows: As above, or in the case of the smaller sizes, see "5th row."
   5th (or last) Row: Place shortest piece of bias along edges of the V, gather and stitch, raw edges of ruffle matching raw edges of V.
4. Sew dart, including raw edges of last ruffle.
5. Across the top add a piece of 1/2in (1.3cm) twill tape or ribbon to finish edge and to form ties or for hook and eye fastening. Tie bustle around doll's waist, centering fullness at back waist.
6. If a fuller bustle is required for a particular style, each ruffle may be slightly stuffed with polyester fiber or cotton before attaching band.

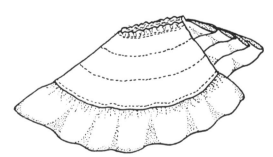

Illustration 26. Wrong side of bustle, showing stitching.

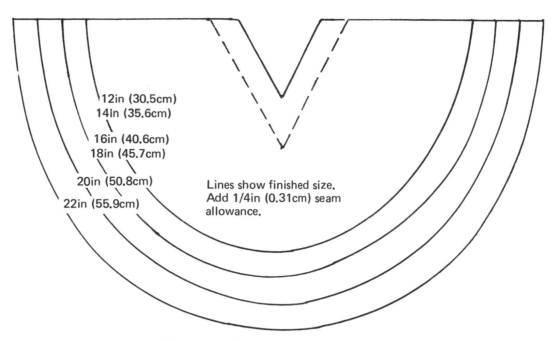

12in (30.5cm)
14ln (35.6cm)
16in (40.6cm)
18in (45.7cm)
20in (50.8cm)
22in (55.9cm)

Lines show finished size.
Add 1/4in (0.31cm) seam
allowance.

Illustration 24. Underwear bustle pattern.

The following chart shows width and length of ruffles needed for each size.

CHART FOR BUSTLE				
DOLL SIZE	WIDTH OF BIAS	NUMBER OF ROWS	LENGTH OF RUFFLES	TOTAL
12in (30.5cm) to 14in (35.6cm)	2in (5.1cm)	3	7in (17.8cm), 8in (20.3cm), 10in (25.4cm)	25in (63.5cm)
16in (40.6cm)	2½in (6.4cm)	4	7in (17.8cm), 8in (20.3cm), 10in (25.4cm), 12in (30.5cm)	37in (93.9cm)
18in (45.7cm)	3in (7.6cm)	4	7in (17.8cm), 8in (20.3cm), 10in (25.4cm), 12in (30.5cm)	37in (93.9cm)
20in (50.8cm)	3½in (8.9cm)	4	7in (17.8cm), 8in (20.3cm), 10in (25.4cm), 12in (30.5cm)	37in (93.9cm)
22in (55.9cm)	4in (10.2cm)	5	7in (17.8cm), 9in (22.9cm), 11in (27.9cm), 13in (33.0cm), 15in (38.1cm)	56in (142.2cm)
FOR ALL SIZES, twill tape or ribbon long enough to fit doll's waist, joining ends with hook and eye, or a bow.				

Illustration 23.

*HINT: Cut one long piece of bias, fold carefully with raw edges matching, machine-stitch along raw edges using large gathering stitch, and cut in correct lengths.

SECTION SEVEN
How To Stitch And Seam

Much time could be spent on a review of the many kinds of stitches which are used for various purposes. However, in this era when we are overwhelmed with more activities than our overfilled days permit, it seems unlikely that many of us will find time to engage in intricate hand-embroidered trim. We have listed a few decorative stitches which might be particularly useful on doll dresses, but which can be performed easily and quickly. Likewise, only two types of seams are described .. French and flat felled .. where fine finish is desired either for appearance or to provide secure joining of sheer fabrics.

1. HEMMING STITCH: to produce a hem with stitches almost invisible. Start with the hem folded on the hemline and the top edge folded 3/8in (0.9cm) (or smaller). Using a number 9 needle and lightweight thread (lingerie thread described in HINTS) secure thread at the point it came out of the turned down hem. Keeping the needle under the fold of the hem, slide it on to the next stitch (about 1/4in [0.65cm]). Pick up one or two threads on the undersection for an almost invisible hem.

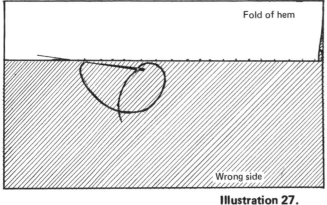

Illustration 27.
Hemming stitch.

2. MORE HEMMING. Pick up one or two threads on undersection (skirt) then slide needle through the fold 1/4in (0.65cm) to the next stitch.

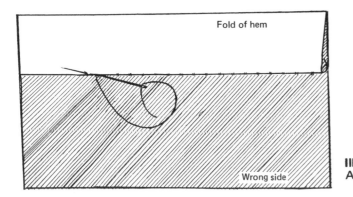

3. WHIPSTITCH: For whipping lace onto folded edge place lace on right side of garment on the folded edge of the hemline, scalloped edge UP. With tiny overcast stitches, attach lace only at the edge of hem. Turn lace down and press gently.

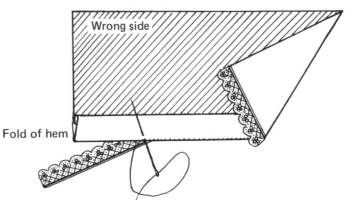

Illustration 29. Whipstitch. For whipping lace onto folded edge. Place lace on right side of garment on fold, with scalloped edge UP. With tiny overhand stitches, attach lace onto edge of hem. Turn lace down and press gently.

4. SLIPSTITCH: Used for attaching cummerbund to dress, for topstitching self-fabric trims, bias trim and so forth. After anchoring needle, slide it in 1/4in (0.65cm) stitches, picking up undersection, then top section, sewing three or four stitches before pulling needle through. When carefully done, *no* stitch will show from right side.

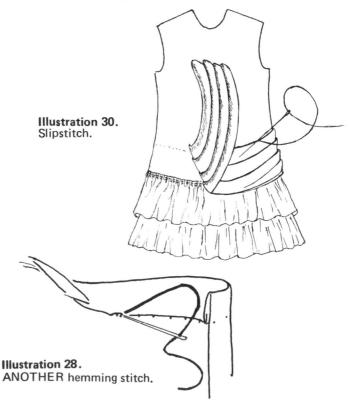

Illustration 30.
Slipstitch.

Illustration 28.
ANOTHER hemming stitch.

5. HANDSEWN LOOP FOR BUTTON OR HOOK. For small buttons handsewn thread loops are much more delicate looking than buttonholes, and the same type loop may be used with hooks instead of using the metal "eye" which is furnished with the hook. To do this use double thread and take two or three stitches back and forth along edge of fold to form a loop. If intended for use with a button, be sure it is large enough to accommodate the button. Buttonhole stitch along the loop, pulling stitch firmly as you proceed. Be sure to secure end of thread tightly because a lot of stress may be put on this loop.

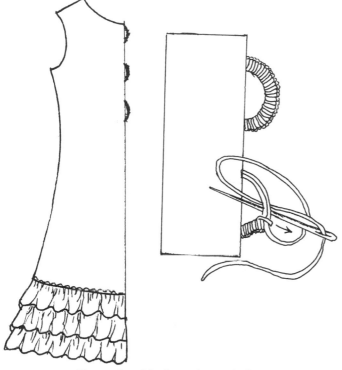

Illustration 31. Loop buttonhole.

6. Attach hook with a single thread, working around the two metal rings with either overcast or buttonhole stitch. Then slide thread around the hook itself several times and secure.

Illustration 32. Attaching hook.

Use buttonhole or overcast stitch around wire rings, and reinforce with several stitches under the wire fold.

SEAMS described here enclose raw edges thus preventing raveling. They can be made very narrow and will add a neat appearance to a small garment.

1. a. FRENCH SEAM. With *wrong* sides together stitch a small seam (1/4in [0.65cm]). Trim very close to stitching. Press seam allowance to one side.

b. Fold on stitch line and stitch a second time from 1/8in (0.31cm) to 1/4in (0.65cm)

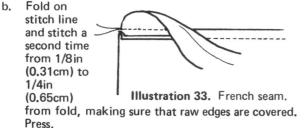

Illustration 33. French seam.

from fold, making sure that raw edges are covered. Press.

2. FLAT FELLED SEAM
   a. With right sides together, stitch a plain seam (1/4in [0.65cm]).
   b. Press seam allowance to one side. Trim the bottom seam allowance ONLY, to 1/8in (0.31cm).
   c. Turn under the top seam allowance, pressing it flat and covering the trimmed side.
   d. Stitch flat, close to folded edge.

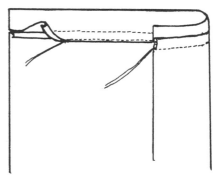

Illustration 34. Flat felled seam.

SECTION EIGHT
How To Do Cartridge Pleating *

Cartridge pleating is a method of pleating a great width of material to be gathered into a small band, as, for example, when dressing a china (porcelain) doll with a tiny waist, when you want a bouffant skirt. Even bulky fabrics can be adapted in this manner to a tiny waistline.

METHOD:

1. Cut a rectangle of fabric correct in length for the doll to be dressed, adding allowance for a 1/2in (1.3cm) turn at the waist and whatever hem is desired. Turn top edge 1/2in (1.3cm) and press.

2. With right side facing you, start close to the fold, using double thread long enough to cover the full length of fabric. Stitch in small basting stitches evenly spaced and about 1/8in (0.31cm) apart across the length of the fold.

NOTE: With practice you will learn to regulate the size of the stitch depending on the weight of the fabric, amount to be gathered and so forth. Keep in mind when you experiment, THE LARGER THE STITCH, THE GREATER AMOUNT OF FABRIC CAN BE DRAWN INTO THE NARROW WAISTBAND. It is a good idea to determine the approximate size of the stitch to be used by dividing the band into four equal parts, the skirt material into four parts. Work with one-quarter until you have a pleasing effect, with pleats softly and evenly spaced along the quarter section of band.

3. Place another row of stitches directly below the first row, matching the stitches exactly.

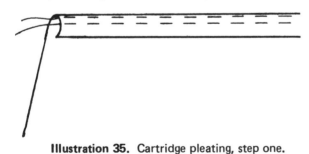

Illustration 35. Cartridge pleating, step one.

4. Pull threads for both rows evenly to the length desired. You will note that you will have the fabric neatly pleated, as in *Illustration 36.*

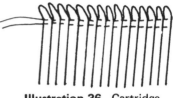

Illustration 36. Cartridge pleating, step two.

5. Attach to the bodice or band by catching only points of the pleats on the RIGHT side of the skirt and sewing to the band with tiny stitches. The inside bulk will add very little fullness to the outside, and the pleating forms a lovely finish on the outside.

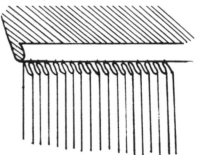

Illustration 37. Cartridge pleating, step three.

EXAMPLE: The following gives dimensions for a skirt for a doll about 16in (40.6cm) to 17in (43.2cm) tall. Practice with this size will give you a good idea of proportions.

1. Cut a piece of material 13in (33.0cm) x 38in (96.5cm) on straight of cloth, this measurement allowing for the 1/2in (1.3cm) turn at the top, and a 2in (5.1cm) hem. Turn and press 1/2in (1.3cm) at the top.

2. Cut a piece of fabric for band 1¼in (3.2cm) wide and 1¼in (3.2cm) longer than the waistline of the doll. Fold ends 1/2in (1.3cm) forming center back placket. Sew as directed for pleating.

*This is also referred to as "organ pleating" or "gauging."

SECTION NINE
How To Flute Without A Fluter

Fluting looks somewhat like fabric slightly crimped or in tiny waves. It can be used on self-fabric to enhance the appearance of the dress, is a pleasant variation from tiny pleats and can be used on most kinds of cotton lace providing they have enough body to steam into folds.

One advantage to the use of fluting is the control of fabrics which might otherwise tend to stand out from a dress instead of lying flat or hanging as one would expect it to appear on a child's dress or an adult dress. Even a tiny ruffle of lace treated in this manner will hang properly instead of "sticking" out and spoiling the contour of the dress. On tiny cuffs one can also achieve a completely controlled look.

METHOD:
1. Decide on the width of the ruffle needed. Cut a length about two and one-half times the length of the area to be covered by the ruffle. Hem one long end of ruffle, the tiniest possible hem. (Some machines have an attachment which will produce a 1/16in [0.15cm] hem, finer than is usually possible when working by hand.) Run gathering thread, either by hand or by machine, across the top edge of the ruffle.
2. Get out the ironing board, a ton of pins (more or less!) and a steam iron. Starting with one end of the ruffle pin into the ironing board at the top and bottom of ruffle with pins at a slightly outward angle. Lift ruffle slightly to form a tiny scallop, and pin in scallop at both top and bottom edges.
3. Repeat this every 1/4in (0.65cm) lifting the material between each set of pins, and using about 1/2in (1.3cm) of fabric to form little scallops. At both top

and bottom edges catch as little of the material as possible, only every two or three threads. Be sure to keep the straight grain of fabric between pins. Continue this until all the material is used or you run out of ironing board space!
4. Hold a STEAMING iron over the pinned area, hovering close to fabric but NOT touching it. Hold iron over fabric for about ten seconds. LET DRY BEFORE REMOVING PINS. Continue on to remaining length of ruffle. When ready to apply ruffle to garment, gently pull gathering stitches until ruffle fits the garment, and sew in place by hand.

Lace treated in this manner can be used on the brims of bonnets, on cuffs of dresses, down fronts, or where ever ruffling or pleats are attractive. This lovely fluted ruffle will, if carefully handled, remain in place forever... or almost forever.

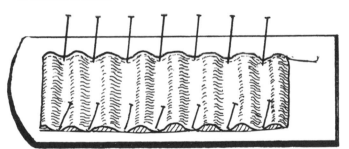

Illustration 38. Fluting on an ironing board.

SECTION TEN
All About Bias

The following information about bias cuts and their uses was copied from a student's workbook of 1909, and while it contains more information than is generally needed now, we felt that it might, nevertheless, be of interest. The use of bias cut fabrics is still as stated in these notes and indicates that the use of bias in this way adds an authentic touch to the trim on your doll garments.

We have added our own notes and illustrations about uses for bias, to assist in cutting, joining and otherwise using bias.

FROM A STUDENT'S NOTEBOOK 1909.

"NOTES ON THE THEORY AND USES OF THE *BIAS*"

"In order to make garments fit the form or to give them more desired shape, biasing edges and seams are used. Such places are represented in patterns by *slanting lines* as distinguished from the vertical and horizontal lines that may be there. In the garments these slanting lines will be found to cut the warp and woof threads of the material at various angles. The kinds of angles formed serve to classify the various biases. There are 3 such biases. I.E.

1. When the slanting line cuts both the warp and the woof threads at the same angle, a *true* bias is formed and is equal to an angle of 45 degrees.
2. A *half bias* is formed when the slanting line gives an angle with either the warp or woof thread, which is exactly one-half of the true bias, and is equal to an angle of 22½ degrees.
3. Any angle made with either warp or woof thread which is larger or smaller than a true bias and yet is not a one-half bias, is called a *choice* bias. It is the one most used in the making of garments.

A true bias is seldom used in the larger portions of garments, but is much used for folds, facings and ruffles; or for decorative effects - - when an entire garment is cut from a plaid or striped material, or when a yoke or front is cut on the bias. It is also used where a gore of a skirt or another part has to be 'pieced' in order to get the desired shape or size. A one-half bias is often found on the side gore of a very flaring skirt, or one with four gores as is a petticoat; is sometimes found at the centre back of a skirt, in sleeves, etc., but is not as common as the choice bias - which allows us to fit or shape the garment we like . . .

Any biasing line may be curved either out or in from the exact line forming the bias, when the seam is to make the garment fit some curved portion of the form - as - at the elbow, shoulder, underarm, or over the hips to give a ripple at the bottom of the skirt.

Any biasing seam must be very carefully handled, or it will stretch badly. First, indicate the cutting line on the material by a traced line of some sort as one made with the tailor's chalk, pencil, tracing wheel or by scoring with the dull side of a pair of scissors. Do *not* indicate the cutting line by a fold. Do *not* lift up from the cutting table or put the hand under the material while cutting any biased edge. Before sewing the seam must be carefully basted with a rather fine basting stitch and held as loosely as possible in the hand while working. If a biasing and a straight edge are to be joined, hold the biasing edge *toward* you while sewing and if possible do not work against the cut threads.

Whenever possible a straight edge and a biasing edge should be joined as then the straight edge will help to keep the biasing one from stretching. This rule is best shown in putting a skirt together, the only place in this garment where two biasing edges need join is at the middle of the back . . .

The best seam to use is the felled, especially if both edges are biasing - as usually happens under the arm of a nightgown, back of a petticoat or skirt, shoulder or underarm seams. On an outside garment this seam would, of course, show the stitches too plainly on the right side to make it always desirable, and in this case, the french seam is the next best to use, or, on heavy woolen material, the common seam, strengthened with a tape or binding ribbon could be used, or it may be "welted." These methods prevent stretching of the seam."

So there you have a touch of the past, surprisingly just as relevant to the use of bias cut fabric now as it was then.

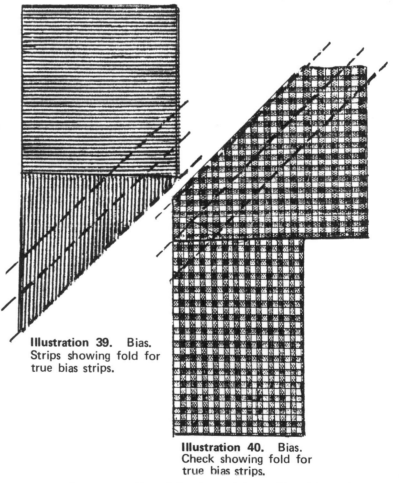

Illustration 39. Bias. Strips showing fold for true bias strips.

Illustration 40. Bias. Check showing fold for true bias strips.

As was mentioned in the article on bias, bias strips make interesting trim. *Illustrations 39 and 40* show how plaid and striped bias look when you are preparing to cut strips. It is easy to see the possibilites in using plaid bias or striped fabrics for a different kind of trim.

We add the following information about bias as we see it.

FRENCH BIAS: Cut a *true bias* somewhat wider than regular bias (as for example 2in [5.1cm] instead of 1½in [3.8cm]). Fold carefully, holding raw edges together with long basting stitches. Lay on garment edge to be bound or faced, basting 1/4in (0.65cm) from raw edge of both garment and bias. If edge is to be bound, gently stretch bias in place, machine-stitch, turn bias and bring folded edge to the stitch line. Hand-sew in place. This method insures a more uniform width. It is also a good method for making a "stand-up" mandarin collar on a doll dress.

For *faced edge* lay bias on right side of garment on edge to be faced, holding in somewhat on a cut or curved edge, allowing fold to lie flat on garment. Sew by machine, *clip seamed* edge at 1/2in (1.3cm) intervals, turn with bias lying flat, and tack folded line of bias lightly. Again with this method, no second turn of bias edge is required and edge is less bulky.

The only difference between this method of applying bias and the more conventional, is that the bias is used in double thickness instead of a single thickness.

HEMMING: To hem bias-cut ruffle, machine-stitch 1/8in (0.31cm) from edge. Trim as close to stitching as possible and follow instructions given above. Hand-hem and you should have a hem considerably smaller than 1/8in (0.31cm).

NOTE: *Illustrations 41, 42 and 43* show how to cut true bias, how to join bias strips, trimming and pressing.

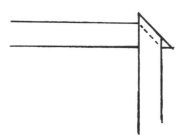

Illustration 42. Bias. Joining bias.

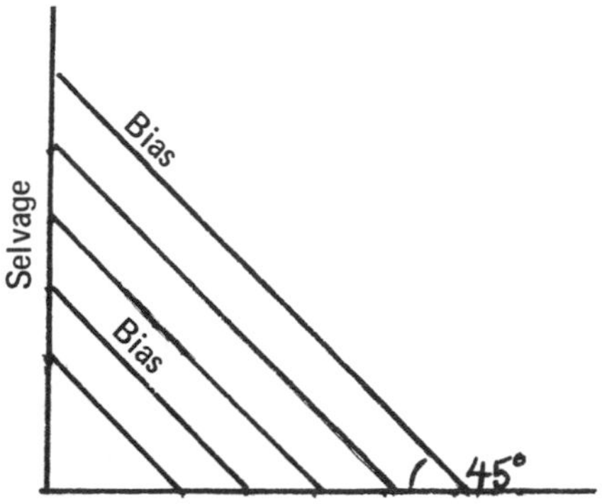

45 degree angle makes true bias

Illustration 41. Bias. Cutting true bias.

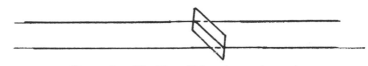

Illustration 43. Bias. Trimming and pressing.

SECTION ELEVEN
How To Tuck For Trim

Tucking appears on old clothes, both for adults and children, on almost any garment worn: on drawers, petticoats, guimpes, yokes and dresses. They are generally small for all kinds of garments, ranging from really tiny (1/32in [0.08cm]) on infants christening dresses, to not more than 1/4in (0.65cm). We suggest 1/8in (0.31cm) tucks for most tucks on doll clothes, particularly those on underwear.

Any of the following are useful techniques from which you may want to select one that appeals to you.

1. a. Mark lightly with pencil along a line 1¼in (3.2cm) from the bottom of a petticoat "rectangle." Fold and press firmly along this line.
   b. Using a small machine-stitch, stitch 1/8in (0.31cm) from folded edge, or use narrow prong of a presser foot as a guide for a narrow tuck. With practice, you may even use one half the width of the presser foot.
   c. Press tuck downward.
   d. Mark a line 1/2in (1.3cm) from folded edge, fold and press. Repeat instructions b and c.
   e. Repeat for as many tucks as are desired. From three to five tucks on doll underwear make attractive trimming - - fine, narrow, uniform and close together.
   f. Bottom edge may then be hemmed, lace attached.
2. To make measuring easier, use a rectangle of cardboard about 1in (2.5cm) by 3in (7.6cm). Figure the gauge you wish to use, cut as shown in *Illustration 44*, and make a tuck marker for uniform marking.
3. Using the aforementioned method it is possible to thus treat a long length of fabric which can then be doubled lengthwise and used to cut matching drawers and petticoat with identical trim. FOR EXAMPLE: Add length of petticoat material and that needed for drawers, and do all the tucking at one time, as well as hemming and adding lace trim BEFORE cutting the garments. See *Illustration 45*. The small amount of wasted material is insignificant compared to the advantage of cutting in this way.

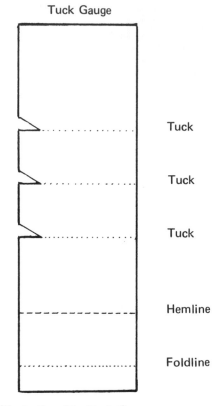

Tuck Gauge

Tuck

Tuck

Tuck

Hemline

Foldline

Illustration 44. Tuck Gauge.

4. TRIM WITH TUCKS.
   SHELL TUCKS: Fold fabric, wrong sides facing, where tucks are desired. Mark dots evenly spaced (for doll clothes from 1/2in [1.3cm] to 3/4in [2.0cm]) apart and with a depth or distance in from the fold of about half the length of the tuck. Make running stitches along tuck. When you reach a dot, take two

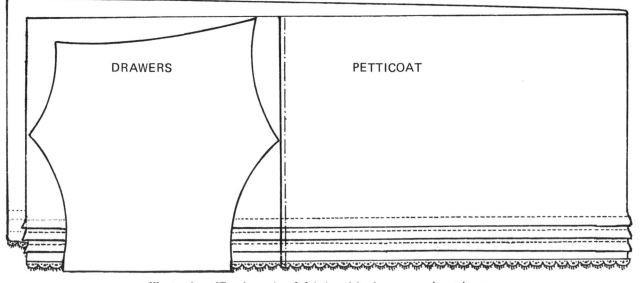

DRAWERS

PETTICOAT

Illustration 45. Length of fabric with drawers and petticoat.

stitches *over* the tuck and pull thread tight to form shell. The double stitch will hold fabric in place. Resume running stitch without breaking thread, and repeat at dots.

Repeat on other garments experimenting with varying intervals depending on the size of the garment. Around skirts where trim might ordinarily be placed, you can make one or two tucks 1/2 in (1.3cm) wide and scallop them. Be sure to align the scallops so one is directly over the other. See *Illustration 46*.

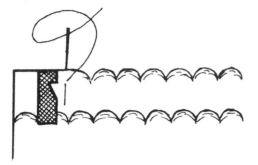

Illustration 46. Tucks scalloped.

5. TRIM with tucks on a blouse or yoke. If you are planning to put tucks in a doll blouse, measure a square or rectangle large enough for pattern with additional for tucks. Sew tucks in place and press BEFORE CUTTING the piece.

Tuck large section. Cut pattern.

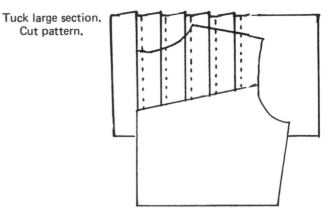

Illustration 47. Yoke tucked and cut.

6. TRIM with crossed-tucks. This is an interesting decorative trim for blouses and yokes. Measure the fabric required. Stitch tucks going in one direction first, and press in one direction. Make a second row of tucks at right angles to the first rows. Hold the first tucks as you stitch the intersecting rows so that they will all lie in the same direction when pressed.

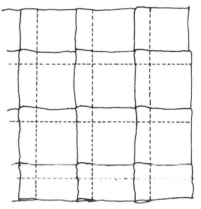

Illustration 48. Crossed-tucks.

SECTION TWELVE
How To Trim With Ruffles

Ruffles are found in profusion on both children's and adults' dresses and so are indispensable in planning for trim on our antique dolls. Making yards of ruffles can be a tiresome process (withal a labor of love), but fortunately the quantity needed for a doll's dress is considerably smaller than for children's garments . . . (or how about some ladies' dresses with elaborate trim that required as much as 150 yards?). Presented here are six variations of ruffling, any one of which can be used effectively to produce a charming finished product.

The choice of one of these methods depends on the fabric you are using, the length of the ruffle and whether the ruffle top is to be covered, or finished with self-fabric or trimming. It is a good idea also to experiment with these methods and select one you most enjoy making and which, at the same time, suits your needs.

Shown here are the six methods mentioned:

1. Use a single thickness of fabric, and hand or machine hem. This is good for heavier fabrics, and has a finished heading. Cut a strip of fabric about 2in (5.1cm) wide and *three* times the length of the area to be trimmed. Hem one edge with a tiny hem, either by hand or machine, or zigzag with narrow stitches close together. Turn down 1/4in (0.65cm) on the other or raw edge. Machine-stitch one row of gathering stitches as close to the folded edge as possible, another 1/8in (0.31cm) from the first row of stitching. Pull threads gently to gather fabric to size, distributing gathers evenly. For long strips, work the fabric gently as thread is pulled; it is possible to work from both ends toward the center to relieve pressure on the thread. (Did you know that on most machines the bobbin thread will pull more easily than the top thread?)

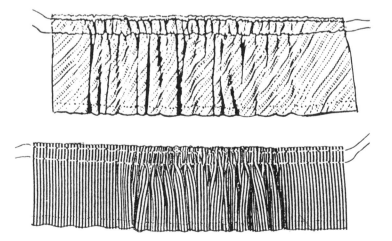

Illustration 49. Ruffle with shirred thread.
Work gathering toward center to relieve tension on thread.

2. Use a double thickness of sheer or lightweight fabric to form a ruffle which requires no hemming and, in addition, may be finished with a narrow ruffled heading. ***Cut ruffle twice the finished width required plus seam allowance (i.e. for a finished width of 1½in [3.8cm], cut fabric 3in [7.6cm] wide plus 1/2in [1.3cm] for seam allowance). Fold with raw edges

Illustration 50. Ruffle - - a tube.

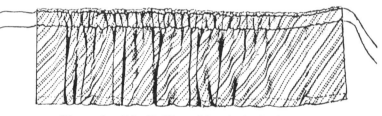

Illustration 51. Ruffle - - bias single thickness.

together (DO NOT PRESS) and stitch 1/4in (0.65cm) from raw edge, forming a long tube. Turn inside out. Lower the seam 1/4in (0.65cm) by sliding into place with finger pressure, leaving a fold at the top. Sew gathering threads just *above* the stitch line and 1/8in (0.31cm) above the first row.

Follow directions in number 1, starred section *. . . . .*. You will have a neat ruffle with no hem showing, and a dainty heading.*** (Reference will be made to this section in a later description of ruffles.)

3. Single thickness, cut on TRUE BIAS, using measurements described in number 1 and shown in *Illustration 49.* Follow instructions for number 1. Advantages are a slightly flared ruffle which need not be quite so full. Patterned fabrics, stripes or plaids, when treated in this way make unusual trim as the bias cut "rearranges" the fabric design for interesting contrast and was often used for this purpose in antique clothes.

4. For double ruffle on sheer fabrics and to avoid hemming, cut ruffle on true bias, again cutting twice the finished width (i.e. for 1½in [3.8cm] ruffle cut 3in [7.6cm] plus 1/2in [1.3cm] seam allowance). Follow instructions starred ***. . . . .*** in number 2.

Illustration 52. Ruffle - - bias doubled.

5. For a ruffle with a *trimmed* heading: Cut 1¾in (4.5cm) wide and hem. Do not turn upper edge, but place two rows of gathering stitches, one 1/4in (0.65cm) from raw edge, the other 1/8in (0.31cm) from raw edge. Gather to fit as in other methods, and tack on dress as desired. Using 1/4in (0.65cm) to 1/2in (1.3cm) insertion lace or ribbon that width, or contrasting material, lay one edge along lower gathering line (covering stitching) and blindstitch. Blindstitch the top edge to complete trim.

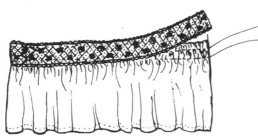

Illustration 53. INSERTION - - trim over raw edge.

Colored ribbon may be placed under insertion lace for a really lovely finish, or colored ribbon may alone supply the trim. Advantages are ease of preparation and attractively trimmed heading, with many kinds of color contrast possible.

6. CORDED RUFFLE. Ruffling may be sewn over cording using a cording foot, or it may be done by hand, being sure not to catch cording in the stitching as the cording will be pulled to gather the ruffle. Cut a strip of fabric 1¾in (4.5cm) wide and about three times the length of the area to be trimmed. Hem, then turn raw edge 1/2in (1.3cm) over cord which will then serve as a drawstring and will also provide a nice little "rib" at the top of the ruffle. Pull drawstring cord to fit area to be covered and tack in place. Sometimes thick wrapping string is adequate for a drawstring cord in tiny ruffles of sheer fabric, but BE SURE to shrink the string first.

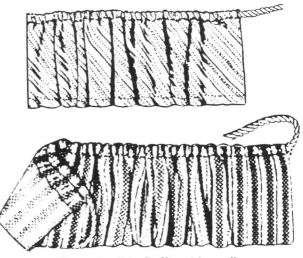

Illustration 54. Ruffle with cording.

SECTION THIRTEEN
How To Cord For Trim

Cording on antique garments was used at least as early as the 1600s. It is, of course, still used for various purposes, primarily decorative and to give edges a finished appearance. The technique varied very little from that commonly used now, except for the use of smaller size cord and slightly narrower bias on the small garments.

Cording may be used around necks, armseyes, and wrists, down fronts of dresses with inserted vests, and around waists, to name only a few places. The method suggested here is used to reduce the bulk of regular cording which, if used on doll clothes, would result in a thick ridge of cloth under the neckline. This method may be confusing at first but practice will simplify the method and it is well worth the effort. Also when cording is applied in this manner, cording and facing are completed in one operation.

TWO METHODS OF APPLYING CORDING, with same end result.

1. a. Cut bias of the length required and 1¼in (3.2cm) wide. Fold about 1/4in (0.65cm) along one edge; insert cord and sew by hand or by machine using zipper foot as close to cord as possible.

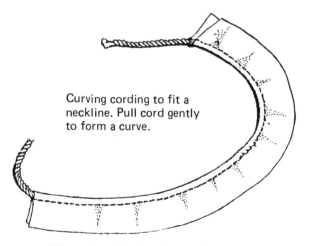

Illustration 55. Making cording.

b. Pull cord gently until material almost forms a circle, but do not allow any puckers along the corded edge. (See *Illustration 56*.)

At this point you may choose one of the two following methods of applying the cording which you have prepared.

METHOD A. After cording has been pulled to form a curve (almost a circle), set it on the staystitch line already sewn around the neckline, cord facing downward as one would apply bias tape, right sides together; cut edges almost matching and stitch on the stitched row used to hold the cord in place. Turn bias to wrong side of garment, thus turning cord upward along neckline with raw edges of bias toward the inside of the garment. Turn raw edges under and hem flat by hand.

METHOD B. If you want to see what you are doing instead of working "blind," proceed as follows: Turn neck opening down 1/4in (0.65cm) (on staystitch line) toward inside of garment using the staystitch line as a fold line. Baste LOOSELY to fold. Place cording inside of garment with cord UP so that only the cord shows from right side of the dress. Blindstitch enough to hold in place. REMOVE loose basting. (Now you can see exactly how the finished work will look - - you can

Curving cording to fit a neckline. Pull cord gently to form a curve.

Illustration 56. Curving cording to fit.

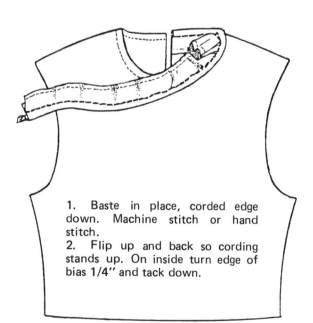

1. Baste in place, corded edge down. Machine stitch or hand stitch.
2. Flip up and back so cording stands up. On inside turn edge of bias 1/4" and tack down.

Illustration 57. Applying cording to neckline. Method A.

verify the size of the cord on the neck edge, and make sure that none of the machine stitches show.) Check on doll for fit. If satisfactory, sew with small hand stitches permanently over blindstitch. Turn raw edges under and hem flat by hand. If a tiny ruffle of lace is desired, it may be sewn by hand directly onto bias on the wrong side of the garment.

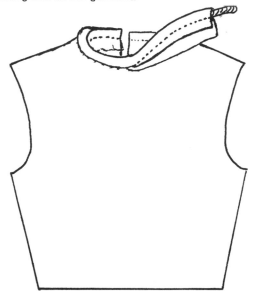

Illustration 58. Applying cording to neckline. Method B.

Work from right side, tucking the corded edge into neckline.

1. Turn down to inside on staystitch line.
2. Set cording on inside, corded edge up.
3. Tack cording loosely to fold of staystitch line, and blindstitch.
4. Try on doll. If fit is good, reinforce over blindstitch. Secure on inside.

TRIM WITH CORDING. Beautiful trim may be made by cutting a strip of material double the length to be trimmed and 1½in (3.8cm) wide. Cord both edges, turning down about 3/8in (0.9cm). Use cording as a drawstring along both edges, pulling gently to fit garment. Pull to straighten grain crosswise and tack on garment. Slight gathers and corded edges make attractive simple trim, usually of self-fabric.

Illustration 59. Cording trim.

SECTION FOURTEEN
How To Work With Lace

Probably the most important area of trim on antique fashions is the lavish use of lace. Certainly old lace has a quality unmatched for use on doll clothes, but not everyone has a source for some of the delicate and beautiful lace which used to be available (expensive even then) nor are laces easy to find now. With the advent of synthetic fabrics, the manufacture of cotton and silk laces dwindled. We would guess that 90 percent of the lace now sold is at least partly synthetic, whereas we really need all-cotton laces for authentic trim on doll garments. Again the doll costumer looks to flea markets and old garments for cotton laces and for variety which may not be found elsewhere.

The use of lace is so integral a part of sewing doll clothes that many pages could be devoted to the subject. However, we are confining our discussion to a few techniques that we have found particularly useful for doll clothes. You will also find useful many of the references to lace in the section "Hints."

The following are a few ways of using lace which might be new to you and useful for adding color and interest to your doll costume.

INSERTION LACE

1. Use insertion lace with ribbon under it for contrast in color and texture.

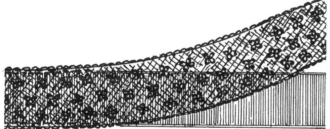

Illustration 60. Sewing insertion lace.

2. Using 3/4in (2.0cm) to 1in (2.5cm) insertion, pleat in tiny pleats (1/4in [0.65cm] to 1/2in [1.3cm]) and use for trim on dresses or around inside and top of bonnet brim. Also consult section on tucking and ruffling for other ways of treating lace.

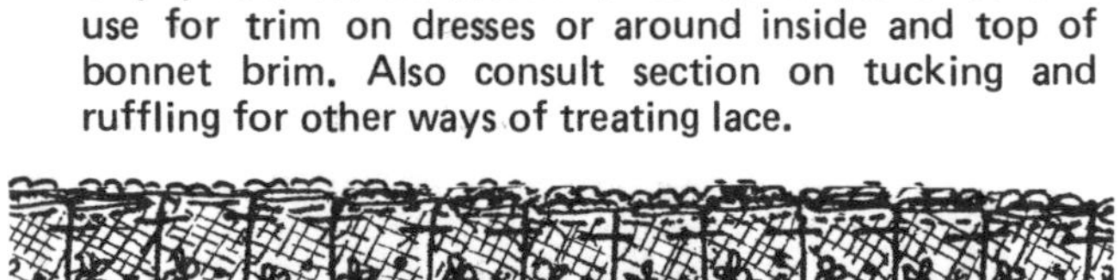

Illustration 61. Pleating insertion lace for trim.

3. Sew insertion on by hand for bands of trim, then to achieve color contrast, run Perlene floss number 9 through mesh at the edges using a tapestry (blunt point) needle.
4. Use one row of insertion added to a row of lace to widen lace as needed.

Illustration 62. Sewing insertion onto lace to widen it.

5. To sew on bands of insertion, lay insertion on fabric and whipstitch in place. It is possible to use very fine machine-stitching also, the short stitch melting into the lace heading.

Illustration 63. Sewing insertion.

6. To achieve a "transparent" look when using insertion, lay on fabric as mentioned previously, and sew in place. Then, turning to the wrong side of the garment, cut through center of fabric backing the insertion (be careful not to clip the lace), press back the fabric to reveal the insertion, trim fabric to 1/8in (0.31cm) and overcast.

Wrong side

Illustration 64. Sewing insertion for transparency.

Turn work over and clip backgrond fabric leaving 1/8in (0.31cm) at each edge for turning.

Turn edges and sew flat, exposing insertion lace. Tack edges in place.

WAYS OF USING EDGED LACE

1. Back lace with colored silk for color contrast.
2. Attach lace to English net to extend width of the lace or to make gathering less bulky.
3. Use wide lace gathered around a high neck of a dress to form a lovely collar. Two rows may be used, the under piece being somewhat longer than the top row for a tiered effect.
4. Lightly gather lace over self-fabric ruffles.
5. Pleat as noted in number 2 above and shown in *Illustration 61*, and use at wrists for simple cuffs. Lace may be turned upward or downward and embellished at sewing line with fine braid or edged with an embroidery stitch.

6. Gather onto hem of petticoat and drawers.
7. Stitch straight onto hem of petticoat and drawers. If you plan to do this, consult "Pressing Hint" for pressing lace into a slight curve which gives a little flair to the straight edge.

LAUNDERING LACE

Old lace continually appears in odd places such as old trunks, flea markets, and other places, but often in a terrible state, stained and dirty, torn and darkened with age, but it can be salvaged with care. Use the following system to wash narrow lace without having a curled and stringy mess, a method which was taken from an early 19th century reference.

1. Find a large bottle such as a quart jar or a gallon jug.
2. Use as it is, or perhaps cover with a dampened cloth. Wrap lace around it carefully, layer after layer, keeping edges flat.
3. Set bottle with wrapped lace in soapy water and soak overnight.
4. Dunk up and down in clean soapy water until it appears to be clean. Rinse well, absorbing some of the excess moisture by wrapping in a turkish towel. Let dry. Remove carefully. Lace should be clean and flat. Touch up with a warm iron if necessary.
5. LIGHTENING LACE. If lace is discolored, it may be lightened by dipping it quickly into a weak solution of bleach in warm water, checking with each dip to see if the color is satisfactory. Care must be taken that lace is not completely whitened, which detracts from the appearance of old lace, and that it is not immersed in the bleach solution for very long because the solution might cause deterioration.
6. To restore lace to a somewhat "old" look, or to treat white cotton lace to be used on old garments, it can be dipped in a solution of instant coffee until the desired color is obtained, keeping in mind that that color will be considerably lighter when the lace is dry. A small quantity of lace to be so treated can be wrapped around a glass jar, dunked in the coffee solution, rinsed a little and allowed to dry on the jar. Almost no ironing will be necessary.

How To Use Ribbon For Trim

As with lace, ribbon also follows the same pattern. The soft and incomparable beauty of silk ribbon cannot be found now except at great cost. Since many dresses and bonnets require yards and yards of lace and ribbon trim, we have tried to present some alternatives in both areas. Be sure to refer to lace and ribbon HINTS which will enable you to use fabrics which you already have or to develop colors which are otherwise unobtainable. We have, of course, included ways of handling ordinary ribbon, too.

Ribbon can be used in many ways other than the traditional dress bows and sashes, and bonnet ties. It serves as bright spots of trim, and can be combined with lace in interesting ways, providing trim for a variety of uses. And if you cannot find exactly what you want or need, here are instructions for making your own.

MAKING RIBBON FROM FABRIC

Make your own ribbon as follows, possibly to obtain a self-fabric sash for a dress or the exact matching color for a bonnet: Decide upon the desired width needed, and cut a long strip, trimming the edges carefully. With thread matching the fabric, use a machine to zigzag along both edges with narrow zigzag for which the stitch has been set very close together (almost a satin stitch for which many sewing machines now have an attachment).

Thread of a color slightly contrasting to the color of the fabric will provide a touch of interest. This is particularly nice for wide sashes, which may then be fringed at the ends.

Illustration 65. Self-fabric ribbon bow.

You may have a piece of very wide silk ribbon which, in that form, is not suitable for small dresses. This can be treated in the same way, zigzagging a predetermined width for the garment on which you are working. Even wide velvet can be treated in this way to provide narrow widths for trim. The following methods will provide a variety of trims for all of the uses previously mentioned. "Try them, you'll like them."

1. Use ribbon under insertion to obtain color or texture contrast. See *Illustration 60.*
2. Make fringe by cutting the selvage off ribbon and fringing to desired width for trim around dresses, skirts and hats. It will be delicate and soft.
3. ROSETTES:
   a. To make rosettes of ribbon for small shoes, select a 6in (15.2cm) length of narrow ribbon (1/4in [0.65cm] to 3/8in [0.9cm]) in the color required. Stitch ends together (optional) and run fine hand stitches along the selvage and pull gently until ribbon curls into a corkscrew. Form this into a little rosette and secure on the underside. If you did not stitch ends* together, be sure they are tucked in and out of sight.
   b. Use 3/4in (2.0cm) ribbon, placing gathering stitches 1/4in (0.65cm) from selvage and pull tight. This will provide a double fluted edge. Secure as in number 3.

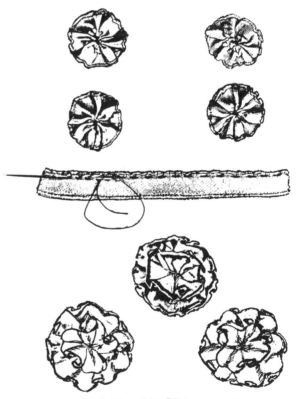

Illustration 66. Ribbon rosettes.

RIBBON BRAID TRIM

Ribbon shirred with any of the following patterns of stitching will produce delightfully different designs to be used on the skirts of fashion dolls, bodices, or for any other spots where braid trim might be suitable. Using ribbon about 1/4in (0.65cm) to 1/2in (1.3cm) wide, sew in any one of the following patterns:

*Touch ends with white glue to prevent raveling.

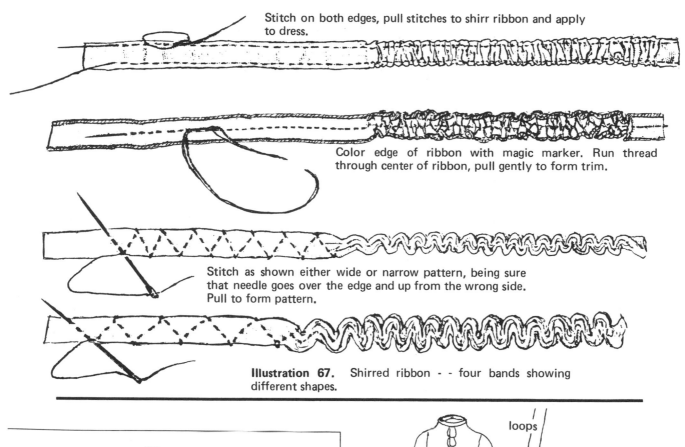

Stitch on both edges, pull stitches to shirr ribbon and apply to dress.

Color edge of ribbon with magic marker. Run thread through center of ribbon, pull gently to form trim.

Stitch as shown either wide or narrow pattern, being sure that needle goes over the edge and up from the wrong side. Pull to form pattern.

Illustration 67. Shirred ribbon - - four bands showing different shapes.

Illustration 68.

A little practice with any of these methods of handling ribbon and varying the types and widths of ribbon will yield innumerable trims to be used with any type of doll costume . . . particularly useful, however, when used on elaborately dressed fashion dolls.

The dress (in *Illustration 68*) shows lavish use of shirred ribbon trim with delightful results.

Any of the shirred ribbons in *Illustration 67* may be used as shown on this dress, but may also be used plain as we show in the following three examples of dresses. It would be possible to apply one of the shirred ribbons on *Illustration 70,* but all three are attractive methods to use as shown.

loops

Illustration 69. Ribbon trim on dress.

Dress front trim. Arrange narrow ribbon in loops, starting from the hemline and working upward, in loops 1in (2.5cm) to 2in (5.1cm).

Illustration 70. Ribbon trim on dress.

Arrange narrow ribbon diagonally in rows down the front of an A-line dress over a contrasting panel. Bows can be added separately after banding is sewn on.

Illustration 71. Ribbon trim on dress.

Add ribbon trim as shown. Bright ribbon may be used in this way with an overlay of insertion. Again, bows may be added separately. This dress would be stunning with one of the shirred ribbon trims.

SECTION SIXTEEN
How To Pleat

Pleating is an integral part of fashions of almost any era, but it was particularly useful and popular in the 1800s, not just supplying fullness in skirts, but as intricate trim around sleeves, necklines, hemlines and bustles. Pleating of this sort is not to be confused with cartridge pleating (See page 82 and *Illustrations 35, 36 and 37*). We are reviewing the basic types of pleating which characterize garments of the 19th century, hardly different from pleating of today. These types of pleating may be used as mentioned for providing fullness in skirts, but reduced to a fine scale will also be found typical of the pleats used in all kinds of trim.*

Three basic types of pleating are:

1. KNIFE PLEATING. Pleats are laid in one direction with the fold of a new pleat just meeting the underfold of the preceding pleat, to form a solid row of overlaid fabric. They may also be formed with space between individual pleats. These overlapping folds may be very tiny, or quite large, although for our purposes wide pleats would rarely be used. Pleats may face all to the right or all to the left, or at center front and center back may turn away from a center box pleat or a center inverted pleat.

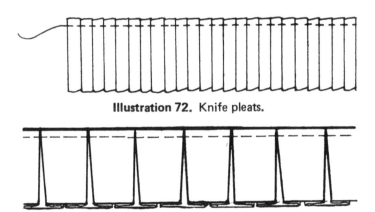

Illustration 72. Knife pleats.

Illustration 73. Symmetrical box pleats.

2. BOX PLEATS. These two straight pleats which face outward to form a panel, are often used all around a skirt. This type of pleating is frequently found on children's hat brims, particularly on the so-called "mobcap" bonnet. This type of pleating can be varied in many ways by adjusting the size of pleats. Illustrations show symmetrical box pleats, box pleats that are uneven, inverted box pleats, and a combination of the two.

*See LACE, p. 92 *Illustration 61*

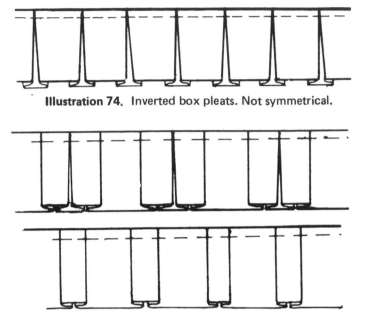

Illustration 74. Inverted box pleats. Not symmetrical.

Illustration 75. Combination of box and inverted pleats.

3. INVERTED PLEATS. This is the opposite of box pleats since the "box" is on the underside of the garment. If box pleats are used on a length of fabric, they actually are alternated with inverted pleats.

PLEATING AS TRIM: One effective trim is produced by fine pleating a narrow length of fabric (1/4in [0.65cm] pleats laid close together) with one edge hemmed or zigzagged, the other turned down 3/8in (0.9cm). Pleating may be sewn on the garment by machine 1/4in (0.65cm) from the folded edge, or even better, sewn by hand, making sure that the edge of each pleat is secured. Then each little corner *above* the stitching is turned down to form a triangle and tacked in place.

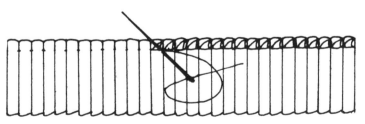

Illustration 76. Pleats with special trim.

SECTION SEVENTEEN
How To Make A Pleater

(Reprinted here from *Costume Quarterly For Doll Collectors* by courtesy of Helen Barglebaugh and May Wenzel.)

"Knife, box and combination pleats play an important part in the eighteen-seventies costume when high fashion decreed pleating be used at neck, sleeve, over and about basque, on overskirts and at hemlines, too.

Demand for precision pleating sent the inventors to drawing boards to dream up the many weird-looking but ingenious contrivances that were later patented.

After using a number of these antique "plaiting machines" the rod type seemed most versatile and easy to use. We finally developed two variations of this form of pleater from simple materials.* Pleater pictured . . . uses one length of 3/4" wood shelving, 3-ounce box of 1" 18-gauge wire brads, 13 threads to the inch needlepoint canvas, approximately 1½ yards of 1/2" elastic, unhemmed padding made of one flannel and one muslin layer, and 120 18-gauge steel rods.

row on long edge. Pad center of board with muslin and flannel . . . .** The method of pleating . . . Working from left to right place a rod over fabric in second space. With another rod, pick up fabric to the right by slipping rod under fabric. Draw rod and fabric to left and place rod in first space. Each set of rods forming a single pleat should be fastened under elastic. For next pleat, repeat with rod over fabric in fourth space; pick up fabric to right with rod underneath; draw to left over rod in fourth space and place in third space; continue until end of board . . . (is reached).

Cover pleated fabric and rods with cloth for steam or dry pressing. When steam pressed, allow to dry before removing rods. Resume pleating by aligning last made pleat in first set of rods at left; continue as above.

Practice plain knife pleating on ribbon to gain rhythm and then graduate to box and combination pleating.

When finished, pleats made on a rod-type pleater have a soft, rounded edge fold. Keep all pleats in position with loose tacking from fold to fold on wrong side."

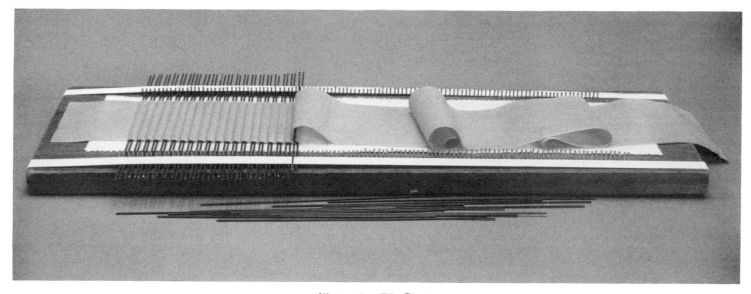

Illustration 77. Pleater.

To make this pleater, cut needlepoint canvas to board face size. Carefully align canvas cut edges along board and secure with masking tape. Mark position of brad row 3/4" from each long edge on the open weave canvas. Also mark position of the first brad for top and bottom row. To drive brad straight, hold it in position with tip of long nose pliers while hammering. Bent brads are easily straightened with same pliers. Allow 1/4" to 3/8" of each brad to remain above board surface. After all brads are in position, carefully cut and remove threads of needlepoint canvas. Attach stretched elastic to fit firmly outside each brad

*We show here only one of the two pleaters.

**Be sure that your steam iron will fit between the rows of brads.

NOTE: When the desired pleats are quite narrow (such as under 2in [5.1cm]) it is possible to use a double width of fabric and complete two rows of pleating in one operation. Cut fabric four times the width of completed ruffle (for 1½in [3.8cm] pleating, a 6in [15.2cm] wide strip). Determine center of strip and fold raw edges toward center, basting or pressing in place. Pleat according to instructions, and then cut through center where raw edges meet, with the result of two strips of pleating with a folded edge so no hem is required.

SECTION EIGHTEEN
Needlecraft

Many kinds of needlecraft of an intricate nature were known throughout many centuries of decorative trim. It would not be possible to go into the subject of needlecraft except for two exceptions. We have included two types of trim described in *The Delineator* - - smocking, copied from *The Delineator*, August 1888, and tatting from *The Delineator*, April 1892, here shown as they appeared in those issues. For those of you interested in reviving either of these skills, the directions in the next few pages should be most instructive. We felt that it might be of interest to include copies taken from old magazines so that you could work with the authentic "old" methods of performing these two arts, although there can be but little difference in the old and the new.

On one page of the tatting reproduction there are directions for making a child's cap. For some of you who are skilled tatters, it should be no problem to make this cap in a smaller size to fit a doll.

DECORATIVE STITCHING

We would not presume to enumerate all of the decorative embroidery stitches which could be used effectively on doll underwear, petticoats, dresses and outer garments. A few, however, which are simple but attractive are described for you. You will note that the foundation stitch for some of these is the largest stitch on your sewing machine. Any of these used singly or in combination can provide touches of color in perfect scale for your small garments.

DECORATIVE STITCHES
1. BASIC STITCH.
   a. Using the longest stitch on your sewing machine at the point where you want trim, and using thread of contrasting color if desired, stitch one row (or two as noted in b) of stitches. Using from two to six strands of six-strand embroidery floss or perle cotton, whip around or through machine stitches but do not sew through fabric, as shown in *Illustration 82*. Pull loosely, as a loose loop will be more attractive. For many of these stitches a tapestry needle (blunt point) will be easier to work with as it catches fabric threads less easily.

Illustration 82. Basic decorative stitch.

   b. Sew two rows of machine stitches about 1/8in (0.31cm) to 1/4in (0.65cm) apart with rows parallel to each other and stitches matching. Whip separately in matching or contrasting colors, or in design shown in *Illustration 83*.

Illustration 83. Basic decorative stitch with two rows of machine-stitching.

   c. Twisted running stitch. Make a series of running stitches, then whip thread around as shown (a variation of machine-stitch base but much larger) as shown in *Illustration 84*.

Illustration 84. Twisted running stitch.

2. BLANKET STITCH
Work from left to right with thread under the needle. Stitches of even sizes with even spacing may be varied by groups as shown. Edge may then be whipped with contrasting color.

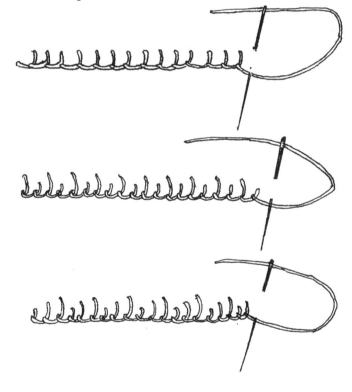

Illustration 85. Blanket stitch.

3. OUTLINE STITCH
Working from left to right, sew a backstitch on line to be trimmed. Take another backstitch, bringing needle out where the last stitch ended, thread always under the needle.

Illustration 86. Outline stitch.

4. CHAIN STITCH

Stitches are placed along a straight line, the thread forming a loop which is held in place by the next stitch.

Illustration 87. Chain stitch.

5. FLY STITCH.

a. Horizontal

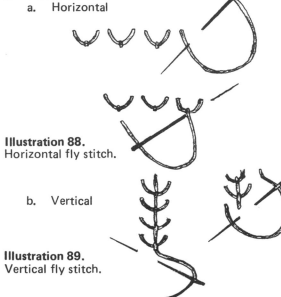

Illustration 88.
Horizontal fly stitch.

b. Vertical

Illustration 89.
Vertical fly stitch.

6. FEATHERSTITCH

This is probably the most characteristic of the embroidery stitches found on infants and children's clothes and on doll clothes to be made in a fine, tiny version. It is obvious that these stitches can be varied in many ways by altering the size of the stitches and the thread used.

a. Single featherstitch.
b. Double featherstitch.

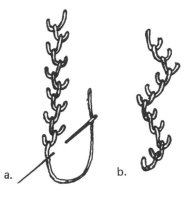

Illustration 90. Featherstitch.

7. FRENCH KNOT

See page 110 and *Illustration 111* for French Knot description.

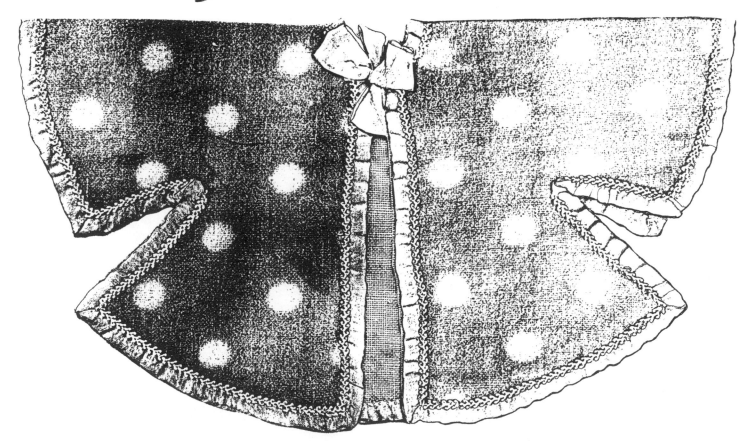

Illustration 91. Doll garment with featherstitch.
Intricate featherstitching on doll garment from 1910, exact size.

SMOCKING OR HONEY-COMBING.
DIRECTIONS FOR MAKING.

The Delineator   **Aug 1888**

Smocking and honey-combing are two titles given a special kind of decorative work that is just now having an extensive vogue. It is seen as much on the garments of grown-up people as on those of the little folks, and is very ornamental in effect,

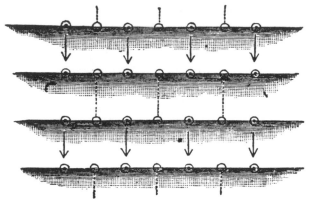

FIGURE No. 1.

illustrates how it may be run to a point when desired. The first thing to do is to space evenly, and this is shown at figure No. 1. The section to be smocked may be creased or marked off in lines with thread or chalk in the direction the smocking is to run, and then on each line dots are made to indicate where the catching together is done. This method will do for all but sheer and delicate-hued fabrics, when marked paper will have to be used as in tucking. Carefully examine figure No. 1; the dots indicated by the arrows are to be caught together in every instance, and those connected by the dotted lines are to be similarly caught. Begin at the topmost space; catch together the dots indicated by the arrows, beginning at the right; insert the needle as shown by figure No. 2, and make the fastening secure, usually two or three over-and-over stitches sufficing; then pass the needle underneath and out through the next arrow dot below, as illustrated at figure No. 3. Continue to the end of the line.

Now begin at the second space and catch together the dots connected by the broken lines, passing the needle underneath and out through the lined dot just below as shown by figure No. 4; then pass the needle through as illustrated at figure No. 5 and make the tacking secure. Each succeeding row is done in the same way. Once properly started the work will not be tedious.

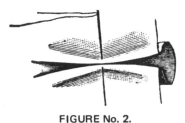

FIGURE No. 2.

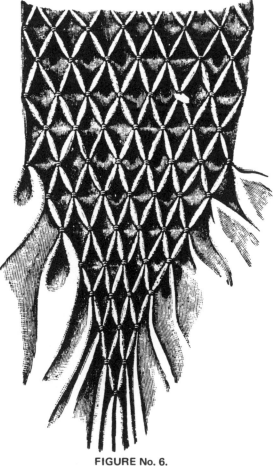

FIGURE No. 3.

FIGURE No. 4.

showing to good advantage on tea-gowns, matinées, breakfast jackets and tennis blouses; it is also introduced in many sleeves and pretty draperies, and even in the coverings of seasonable hats.

The work is clearly explained herein and is not at all difficult of execution, but great care should be exercised in spacing evenly. The style of smocking shown is similar to that used in our patterns of smocked garments. It may be done simply with silk or

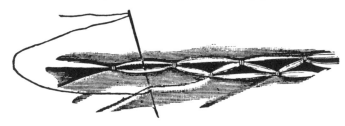

FIGURE No. 5.

cotton, or made more elaborate-looking by sewing in beads at the tackings. The beads may be the same hue as the goods or of a contrasting color, but they should not be large. The material should be soft like cashmere, India silk and similar textures; under the smocking a smoothly-shaped lining is needed, and on this lining is generally a similarly shaped piece of thin crinoline, which imparts the needful firmness. Only the outer edges of the smocking need be caught to the lining, which is added simply to prevent the smocking from stretching.

FIGURES Nos. 1, 2, 3, 4, 5 AND 6.—METHOD OF SMOCKING.—The smocking perfected is shown at figure No. 6, which also

Illustration 78. Smocking. August 1888

FIGURE No. 6.

TATTING.—No. 1.

As frequent requests have been made for designs in tatting, it has been deemed advisable to respond by issuing occasional articles upon the subject. In this, the initial article, we have taken it for granted that those who make or wish to make, tatting are acquainted with the method that has been so long employed, and that they would appreciate a more modern method, especially as by it tatting is more gracefully and rapidly made and with even less exertion than by the now old-fashioned method. With this idea in view, we have prepared engravings of the several movements re-

4. This completes one stitch. By a little practice this method will soon become very easy to a beginner, and a favorite with an expert, who will at once realize its advantages over the older method.

PLAIN TATTING AND PICOTS.

FIGURES Nos. 7 AND 8.—These engravings show how to make and join the rings of plain tatting. The method of making the

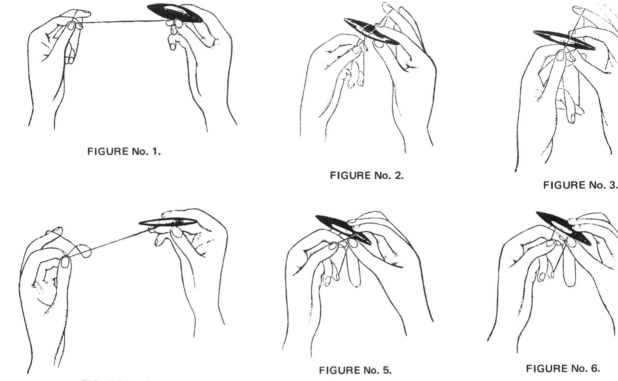

FIGURE No. 1.

FIGURE No. 2.

FIGURE No. 3.

FIGURE No. 5.

FIGURE No. 6.

FIGURE No. 4.

quired for the new method, showing the necessary positions of the hands, thread and shuttle for each detail.

ABBREVIATIONS USED IN MAKING TATTING.

d. s . . . . Double-Stitch or the two halves forming one stitch.
p . . . . Picot.
* . . . . Indicates a repetition as directed wherever a * is seen.

NEW METHOD OF MAKING TATTING.

FIGURES Nos. 1, 2, 3, 4, 5 AND 6.—The first movement, shown at figure No. 1, is the same as that of the older method, the thread being wrapped around the fingers of the left hand to form a circle and brought out from under the thumb. Then the shuttle is grasped as seen in the picture, with the second finger of the right hand between the thread and the shuttle. Now raise the thread with the second finger as seen at figure No. 2, and slip the shuttle entirely *under* it and the circle on the left hand, bringing it back *over* the circle and *under* the lifted thread as seen at figure No. 3. Then, holding the shuttle-thread taut, form a loop of the circle-thread as seen at figure No. 4, drawing it down close to the thumb with the second finger. This forms the first half of the stitch. Now, to make the other half: Hold the shuttle the same as in the first movement, except that you allow the thread to drop loosely down as seen at figure No. 5. Pass the shuttle *over* the circle and bring it back *under* it as shown by figures Nos. 5 and 6; and then pull up another loop (the second half of a stitch) the same as at figure No.

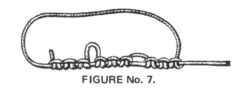

FIGURE No. 7.

stitches has been fully explained; and picots are the long loops seen between the stitches of nearly all designs in tatting.

At figure No. 7 the method of making picots is plainly illustrated the long loop showing how two stitches are divided by it in the formation of a picot. Sometimes picots are made *between* the *two halves* of *one stitch;* but this is not the usual method; the majority of tatting-workers make them between *two whole* stitches as represented at figure No. 7.

Picots are made both for ornament and use. It is by them that the rings of a design are provided with feathery-looking edges and are also fastened to each other. The latter process, together with the plainest complete tatting design made, may be seen at figure No. 8, where a series of rings are joined by picots to form a simple edging. After the last whole ring, the picture shows the next ring begun. Five whole stitches are made, and then the circle-thread is picked up through the last picot of the last ring with a pin, the shuttle thrust entirely through the loop, and the thread drawn taut. Then five more stitches are made; next the center picot; then five more stitches, another picot and five more stitches. Then the circle is drawn down to form the ring, which is sometimes fastened by a knot made something like the joining of picots by picking the thread up through the connecting thread of the last ring

Illustration 79.

with a pin, thrusting the shuttle through the loop thus made and drawing the latter down into a knot at the ends of the ring. Plain tatting is occasionally made without picots and the rings are then separate from each other. Picots may be added in any number or groupings desired. Sometimes they alternate with the stitches across the entire top of a ring; and sometimes but three are made, according to the fancy of the maker or the details of the design.

PLAIN TATTING-INSERTION.

FIGURE No. 9.—It will be seen by this engraving that plain

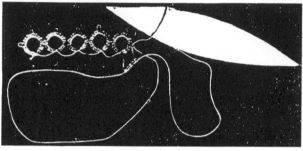

FIGURE No. 8.

tatting and plain tatting-insertion are made upon exactly the same plan, except that the work is turned with every new ring; that is, one ring is first made and then a second one is worked a short distance from it, but the two are not connected. Then the work is turned and a third ring is made and attached by a picot to the *first one,* after the manner illustrated at figure No. 8. Then the work is turned again and a *fourth* ring is made and attached to the *second* one by the method just referred to. Figure No. 9 shows very plainly how the work is joined and progresses.

Tatting may be made of silk, cotton or linen thread or of fine cord, according to the purpose for which it is required. It makes

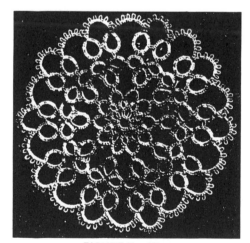

FIGURE No. 10.

very handsome decorations for dresses, underwear, doileys, handkerchiefs, etc.

ROSETTE OF TATTING.

FIGURE No. 10.—This rosette may be worked with fine or coarse cotton, as preferred. It is very handsome when worked in silk for decorating dresses, bags, chair-scarfs, etc., etc.

Begin with the middle ring and work 1 d.s.; then 10 long picots, each separated by 2 d. s., and lastly, 1 d. s.; close in a ring, fasten and cut the thread.

The row following is worked with 2 threads. * Work first with 1 thread only, a ring, as follows: 5 d.s., join to a picot of the middle ring, 5 d. s.; close in a ring and then turn the work and work with 2 threads close to the end of the ring as follows: 5 d. s., 1 picot, 5 d. s.; repeat from * 9 times more, and then fasten the thread to the 1st ring and cut it off.

Next make the circle of three-leaved figures, which are worked separately, but are joined to each other and to the scollops of the preceding round by the picots. Each of the two side-leaves of each figure have 5 d. s., 1 picot, 5 d. s., 1 picot, 5 d. s., 1 picot, 5 d. s.; the middle leaf has 5 d. s., join to last picot of 1st leaf, 7 d. s., join to scollop of middle part, 7 d. s., 1 picot, 5 d. s. The other side-leaf is worked like the 1st one.

The outer row is also worked with 2 threads. Work 1st * a ring

with 1 thread as follows: 14 d. s., fasten to the picot of the 1st or left-hand side-leaf of a three-leaved figure, 7 d. s., 1 picot, 7 d. s.; then turn the work and work with 2 threads 8 times alternately 2 d. s., 1 picot; then 2 d. s.; turn the work and work again with 1 thread a ring as follows: 7 d. s., join to the picot of the preceding ring; 7 d. s., join to the next side-leaf of a three-leaved figure; 14 d. s., turn the work, work a scollop with both threads like the preceding one. Repeat the details from * all round.

FIGURE No. 9.

EDGING OF TATTING.

FIGURE No. 11.—This edging is worked up and down with 2 threads. The rings are worked with 1 thread, and the scollops with 2 threads.

Work as follows: * 1 ring of 7 d. s. (double-stitch), 1 picot, 7 d. s.; turn the work, and with both threads work 1 scollop of 3 d. s., and 5 picots, each separated by 2 d. s.; then 3 d. s., turn the work again and work 2 rings like the preceding, but instead of forming the picot in the first of these rings, join to the picot of the ring already finished; turn the work, make 1 scollop like the preceding, turn, make 2 rings and 1 scollop like the preceding; turn, make 1 ring of 7 d. s., join to the picot of the preceding ring; 7 d. s., turn, make twice alternately, 1 scollop and 1 ring like the preceding ones; join the rings to the same picot to which the preceding ring was joined,

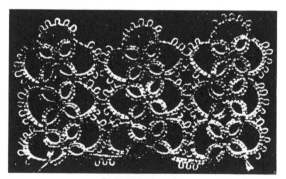

FIGURE No. 11.

so that a figure of 4 connected rings is formed. Now complete the next 2 figures, as yet only half finished, to correspond. After turning the work, make for the upper edge of the edging 1 scollop of 3 d. s., and 3 picots each separated by 2 d. s., then 3 d. s.; turn again and repeat from *, but join the next 3 scollops, instead of forming the middle picot, to the corresponding picot of the 3 scollops last worked. This design, worked in silk, forms a very handsome trimming for vests, cuffs, collars or any dainty fancy-work.

Illustration 80. Tatting.

TATTING.

ABBREVIATIONS USED IN MAKING TATTING.

d. s.—Double-stitch or the two halves forming one stitch.   p.—Picot.   *.—Indicates a repetition as directed wherever a * is seen.

CHILD'S TATTED CAP.

FIGURE No. 1.—This cap can be made of silk, cotton or linen thread, as preferred. Begin the cap at the center of back with a ring of 11 d. s. and 10 p., each separated by 1 d. s.

First round.—This is made of small rings; leave ¼ inch thread and make first ring of 5 d. s. and 4 p. draw up and join to 1st p. of center. Make 2nd round like 1st; join 1st p. to last p. of 1st ring, and continue until you have 10 rings around center; join last ring to 1st, fasten thread under ring and make 6 more rounds like last; join each ring to ring of last round, every 3rd and 4th ring joining 1 p. each of a ring in last round so that the back presents a smooth appearance.

After making 6 rounds of small rings the 7th round is composed of wheels. Make center of 1st wheel of 11 d. s. and 10 p., draw up, leave ¼ inch thread and make 10 small rings of 5 d. s. and 4 p.; join 1st small ring to last small ring of last round. Make 2nd wheel; join 1st and 2nd rings to 4th and 3rd rings of last wheel. Make 3rd ring and join 4th ring to 4th ring

FIGURE No. 1.—CHILD'S TATTED CAP.

ROSETTE IN TATTING.

FIGURE No. 2.—The picots of the center ring of this rosette must each be a quarter of an inch long.

Center ring.—2 d. s., 1 p., * 3 d. s., 1 p. * ; repeat from * to * until there are 10 p., then make 1 d. s., tie, and cut thread.

Outer row.—Use two threads. Begin with one thread and make a ring as follows: 7 d. s., join to any one of the long p. of the center ring, 7 d. s., close ring *. With 2 threads make 3 d. s., 1 p., 2 d. s., 4 p. with 2 d. s. between each, 3 d. s. Turn, and with one thread make 7 d. s., join to next long p., 7 d. s., close the ring *. Turn, and repeat from * to * until the circle is complete.

This rosette, repeated and arranged in points, makes a beautiful design for collars, cuffs, revers, etc.

TATTED STAR FOR HANDKERCHIEF CORNER.

FIGURE No. 3.—Use No. 100 spool cotton. Begin with center ring and make 2 d. s., 1 p., * 4 d. s., 1 p.;

FIGURE No. 2.—
ROSETTE IN TATTING.

FIGURE No. 3.—TATTED STAR FOR HANDKERCHIEF CORNER.

FIGURE No. 4.—
MEDALLION IN TATTING.

of last round; finish wheel like 1st; continue wheels all round. Make 8th round of wheels like 7th. except join the wheels so that they come between the wheels of last round. Make the wheels three-fourths of the way around, thus beginning the front of the cap.

Leave ½ inch thread and return on 9th row with small rings

FIGURE No. 5.—TATTED EDGING.

like center of back. Join 1st small ring to 7th small ring of last wheel; join 2nd ring to 6th ring of last wheel; join each ring to the ring on the sides of wheels across front. Make 10th and 11th rows like 6th round in back. The 12th and 13th rows are composed of wheels. Make 12th row like 7th row, and in the 13th row join the middle side ring of wheels to middle side-ring of wheels in last row. The 14th and 15th rows are like 9th and 10th rows. Make 16th row like 10th row, except you leave 1 inch thread after each ring is joined to last row. These three rows are entirely around the cap. The spaces are to draw ribbon through. Make the last round like 7th round, except that you join them by only 1 ring. Line with silk and add rosettes of ribbon at top and back: also add ribbon ties of the same shade as the lining.

repeat from * until there are 6 picots; then, 2 d. s. and close the ring; draw the thread through p. of ring and make small rings as follows: * 2 d. s., 1 p. and repeat from last * until there are 6 p.; then, 2 d. s. and close ring, and fasten to next p. of ring. Repeat these rings until there are 6, then tie, and cut the thread. Unwind 3 yards of thread from shuttle, and fasten thread to 2 of the picots between the rings; then with double thread make * 1 d. s., 1 p., 1 d. s. and fasten to next p. of rings; repeat from last * to next p., and then make 1 d. s. and 1 p. until there are 9 p. with 1 d. s. between; then, 1 d. s., and fasten to next p.; make * 1 d. s., 1 p., 1 d. s., and fasten to next p.; repeat from last * and fasten to 2 p. between rings. This completes one point.

To Fasten to the Handkerchief.—Make a circle around the points with coarse thread, catching center p. of points. Button-hole stitch with filo silk, and cut out fabric from underneath.

Stars of this description may also be joined the same as medallions to form tidies, doileys, mats, caps or borders.

Illustration 81.

SECTION NINETEEN
About Shoes

Shoes, an integral part of a doll's costume, need special attention to make sure that they blend with the whole outfit, are in character with the costume (i.e. with a walking skirt use boots) and are suitable for the period. However, there is not really much variation in styles of the 1880s to 1890s and in any case most of us are reluctant to have our dolls shod in high-laced or high-buttoned shoes typical of that period. So here we present compromises to children's styles, and look to old dolls to set the fashion.

As we have said before, old shoes are most desirable, so we should make every effort to keep them when we find them on our dolls. The costumer may have to develop some new skills -- become her own "shoe-repairman-in-residence," but the efforts are worthwhile.

The information which follows should be useful for repairing old shoes, restoring trim, or re-covering shoes too dilapidated to use in their original coverings, but from which some parts (such as soles) may be salvaged. Also included are a few simple patterns which may give the ambitious seamstress enough instructions to allow her to make doll shoes "from scratch."

The patterns given here include:
A. Simple slippers in two sizes with instructions.
B. A series of patterns cut from original old shoes showing various trims used. Seam allowances have been added in some cases, but the shoes are otherwise an exact duplicate of the original. Separate instructions are not included as instructions in Section A are adequate.
C. Slippers adapted from an old Jumeau shoe marked
E.J.
DEPOSEE
(Shown on sole, not in scale.)
D. Children's boots. A second upper* is included to be used with the same sole pattern to form a slipper for indoor wear.
E. Shoe pattern (number 11) especially chosen for use with the fold-out pattern for a 20½in (52.1cm) doll is included in this book.
GENERAL INSTRUCTIONS
LEATHER is an ideal medium for shoes as it is pliable and elastic, can be manipulated in small spaces, is compatible with white glue, and is sturdy. Buttonholes can be cut in medium thick leather and do not need reinforcement. However, if fine glove leather is used, it should be lined. For this process note lining instructions in A-2 and A-3. If using heavier leather, ELIMINATE the lining, following instructions excluding references to lining, and cut off seam allowances. Also refer to paragraph marked CUTTING.

FITTING: To insure a proper fit for a specific doll the soles should be cut to fit that doll using the foot for a pattern. Toes may be rounded off or softly curved to a point (see *Illustration 94,* Shoe pattern 3) allowing a fraction all around for "toe space." For the particularly ambitious, buy a chunk of balsa wood at a craft shop large enough to shape with a penknife or an Exacto knife, and make a last** the exact size of the doll's foot and use it for constructing the shoe.

*Upper: the parts of a shoe or boot above the sole.
**Last: a wooden or metal form which is shaped like the (human) foot and over which a shoe is shaped or repaired.

CUTTING: If no lining is being used, trace the upper pattern on the *wrong* side with pen or magic marker and BEFORE CUTTING, stitch with a small stitch about 1/16in (0.15cm) inside the cutting line. (On many machines one-half the width of the presser foot right prong will be 1/16in [0.15cm]). It is not necessary to stitch along the sole line. Cut outside the stitching being sure to keep the margin even all around the stitching.

A. PATTERN AND INSTRUCTIONS FOR A SIMPLE SLIPPER, *Illustration 92* (Shoe pattern 1), for about a 17in (43.2cm) doll, with a small size, *Illustration 93,* (Shoe pattern 2) for a 9in (22.9cm) to 10in (25.4cm) doll.

1. Cut four soles (two inner and two outside) and four heel sections, using cardboard (manila folder is excellent for outer sole, paper pad back for inner sole).

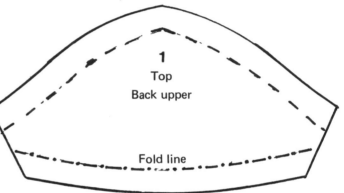

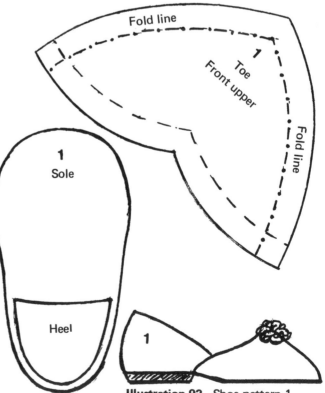

Illustration 92. Shoe pattern 1.

2. Cut two back uppers and two front uppers of fabric or glove leather and the same of unbleached muslin.

3. Place linings on right sides of front and back uppers; sew around edges using 1/4in (0.65cm) seam allowance. Trim. Turn right sides out and press fabric. DO NOT press leather with an iron.

4. Place inner sole on doll's foot or on the last. Starting with the back upper, match CB (center back), fold over the sole 1/4in (0.65cm) and glue. Glue front upper, starting at CF (center front) and overlap side back as shown, again folding 1/4in (0.65cm) at bottom over the sole.

5. Using the outer sole, cover the shoe and raw edge of uppers. If necessary, when fabric is thick, use filler between soles (cotton or additional cardboard).

6. Glue two thicknesses of heel in place on each shoe, or more if higher heel is desired. OPTIONAL: Coat heels and soles with clear varnish, using tip of finger instead of a brush.

7. BOW OR ROSETTE: Cut a strip of fabric 3/4in (2.0cm) by 4in (10.2cm). Fold lengthwise and gather along raw edges, pulling as tight as possible. Fabric will curl into a tight little rosette. Secure with attached thread and attach to shoe at CF. (NOTE: See Shoe Trim, Ribbon, Section 15.)

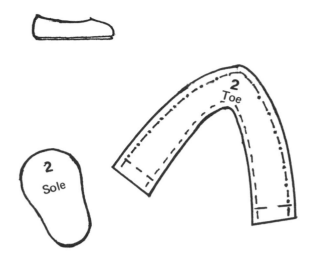

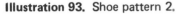

Illustration 93. Shoe pattern 2.

For leather only.
No seam allowance.

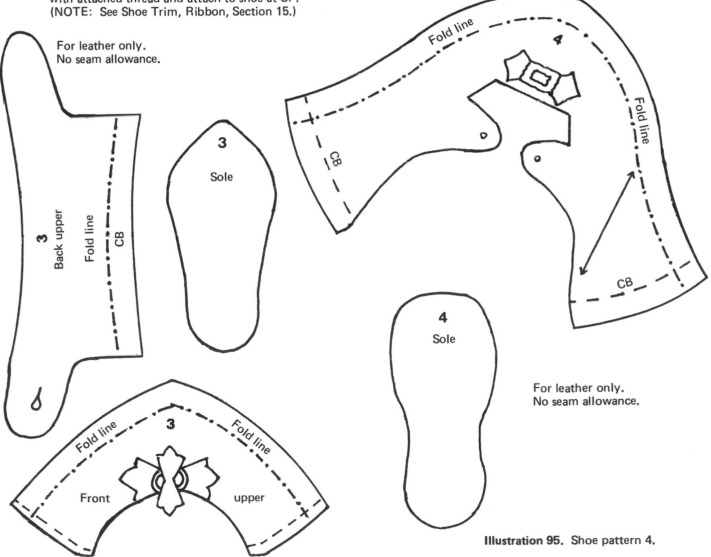

Illustration 94. Shoe pattern 3.

For leather only.
No seam allowance.

Illustration 95. Shoe pattern 4.

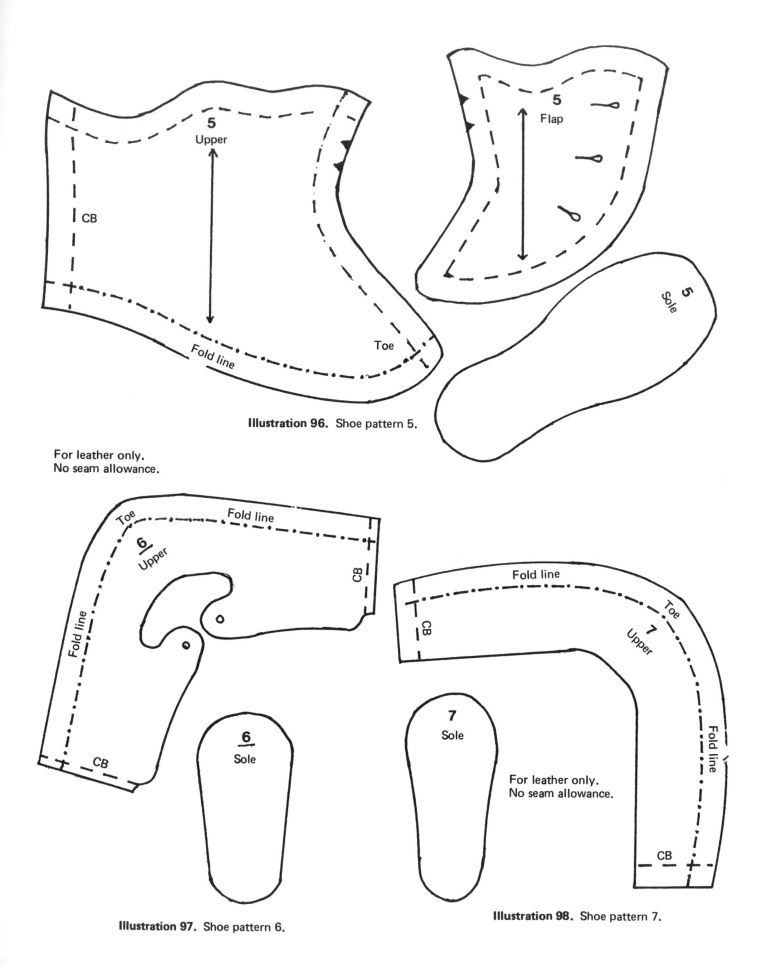

5
Upper

CB

5
Flap

5
Sole

Fold line

Toe

Illustration 96. Shoe pattern 5.

For leather only.
No seam allowance.

Toe   Fold line

6
Upper

CB

Fold line

CB

6
Sole

Illustration 97. Shoe pattern 6.

Fold line

CB

Toe

7
Upper

7
Sole

Fold line

CB

For leather only.
No seam allowance.

Illustration 98. Shoe pattern 7.

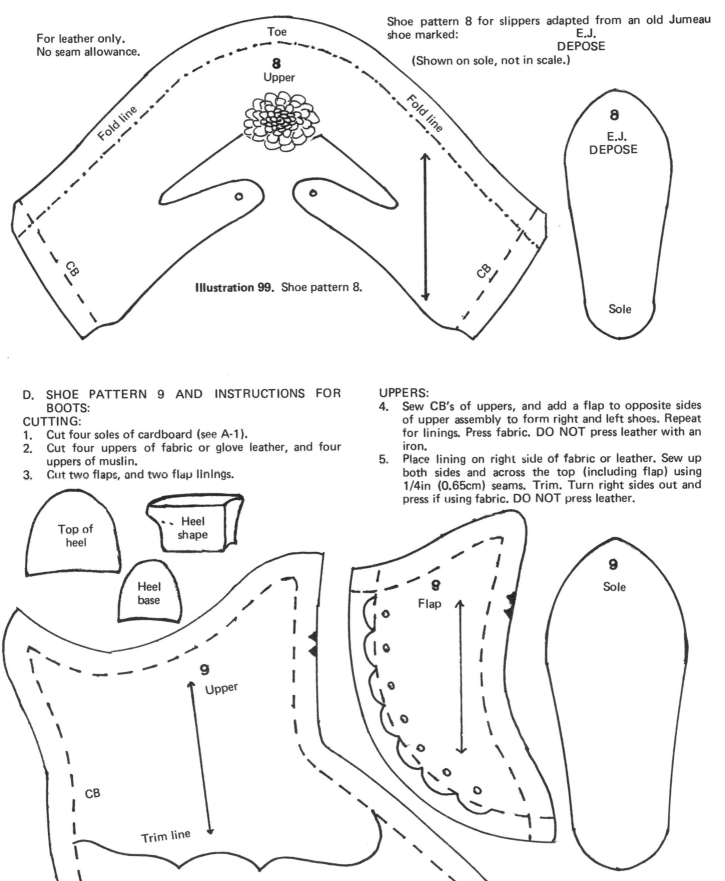

For leather only.
No seam allowance.

Toe

Shoe pattern 8 for slippers adapted from an old Jumeau shoe marked:
E.J.
DEPOSE

(Shown on sole, not in scale.)

8
Upper

Fold line

Fold line

CB

CB

Illustration 99. Shoe pattern 8.

8
E.J.
DEPOSE

Sole

D. SHOE PATTERN 9 AND INSTRUCTIONS FOR BOOTS:

CUTTING:
1. Cut four soles of cardboard (see A-1).
2. Cut four uppers of fabric or glove leather, and four uppers of muslin.
3. Cut two flaps, and two flap linings.

UPPERS:
4. Sew CB's of uppers, and add a flap to opposite sides of upper assembly to form right and left shoes. Repeat for linings. Press fabric. DO NOT press leather with an iron.
5. Place lining on right side of fabric or leather. Sew up both sides and across the top (including flap) using 1/4in (0.65cm) seams. Trim. Turn right sides out and press if using fabric. DO NOT press leather.

Top of heel

Heel shape

Heel base

9
Upper

CB

Trim line

Fold line

Toe

9
Flap

9
Sole

Illustration 100. Shoe pattern 9.

SOLES:

6. OPTIONAL: Turn edges of two outer soles, shaping them around a crochet needle and curve upward. Sand edges slightly upward with an emery board.
7. Place inner sole on doll's foot or last. Fit upper over one sole, starting at CB and CF. Turn 1/4in (0.65cm) over edge of sole. Glue carefully in place. Repeat for other shoe.
8. Glue second sole over each shoe, using cotton or cardboard filler between inner sole and outer sole if necessary.

HEEL:

9. Whittle two heels of balsa wood approximately the shape and size of pattern given. Cover with leather or fabric, pulling taut and gluing 1/8in (0.31cm) fold over top and bottom of heel. Cut to shape and glue cardboard on bottom of heels. Glue heels in place.
10. Sew button loops on flaps as marked to accommodate buttons 3/16in (0.45cm) in diameter. Fit shoe on doll and mark spots for buttons. Sew on buttons.
11. OPTIONAL: Trim as shown in illustration.

SHOE (SLIPPER) PATTERN 10.

Uppers fit sole on Shoe pattern 9 to provide a slipper for indoor wear. The upper could be narrowed somewhat for a daintier style.

THREE-STRAP SLIPPER. SHOE PATTERN Number 11, (*Illustration 102*).

These shoes were especially selected for the fold-out pattern included in this book. The pattern was copied directly from an antique shoe with only minor changes. It is unusual in that there are two ankle straps which close with buttons. A third strap goes over the instep but does not overlap, closing with a button and threaded loop. A decorative bow is attached at center front as seen in *Illustration 103*. Another view shows this shoe with four decorative bows, the three on the straps attached with a button on each side of the straps and slits through the bows for fastening. This is an exact copy of an antique shoe.

INSTRUCTIONS:

1. Place pattern pieces on the wrong side of the leather and draw around the pattern carefully.
2. Place a row of fine machine-stitching just inside the lines of the pattern pieces drawn. Cut on the OUTSIDE of the stitching (on the line drawn).
3. SIDE SEAMS. Place right sides of back and front together and stitch by hand or machine. OPTIONAL: Place two rows of machine-stitching along each side of seam line.

Illustration 102. Shoe pattern 11.

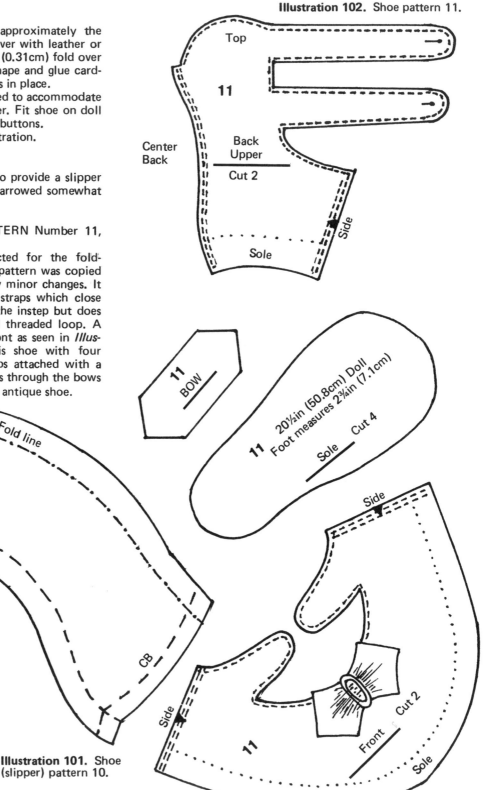

Illustration 101. Shoe (slipper) pattern 10.

108

4. CENTER BACK SEAMS. Sew center back seams, right sides together. Note OPTIONAL stitching in instruction 3.
5. Join instep straps at center front with button and threaded loop. Attach buttons and cut slots for buttons on two highest straps. Buttons are placed on the outside straps of the shoe, buttonholes cut through the leather on the inside straps. OR: Note *Illustration 104* showing the use of four decorative bows on shoe, the upper three fastened with buttons and slits on each side of bow, the fourth sewn at center front.
6. Follow general directions on page 108 for completing soles.

CLOSURES: A variety of methods may be used to fasten shoes, some of which we have listed and illustrated here. Some can be used to advantage on shoes which fit the doll except for straps too tight across the instep.
1. Standard tie across the ankle, but ties may be made of braid, ribbon, or may be crocheted of six-strand embroidery floss in chains of the required length with tiny tassels at each end.
2. Crocheted chains of six-strand embroidery floss may be made to fit across the instep and fastened with a button.
3. One strap fitted over the instep to button on the outside.
4. One strap fitted over the instep and fastened with a buckle.
5. Ornamental strap across instep with a button at each end.
6. One strap coming from center back and attached with a button over the instep (Mary Jane style).

TRIM: Note various shaped bows shown in Shoe patterns 3 and 4, and on *Illustrations 105 through 110.*

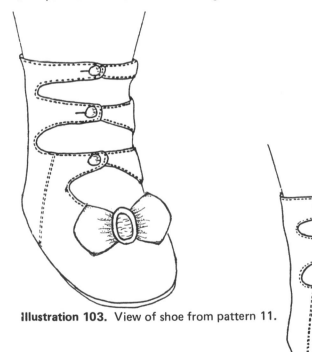

Illustration 103. View of shoe from pattern 11.

SHOE REPAIRS: Here are suggestions for possible repairs to old shoes which might appear fragile but which may well be worth the effort of making repairs to preserve them. Do make the effort before you consider the tattered old shoe fit only for the trash heap.
1. REPAIRING UPPERS: Breaks can be repaired by covering with light layer of white glue on the inside of the shoe and reinforcing with organdy or light-weight unbleached muslin.
2. REPAIRING SOLES: If soles need to be mended, cut duplicates from cardboard (manila folder) using the original as a pattern. Lightly sand the edges and curl a little over a crochet hook, glue on and varnish (only a little varnish is necessary, applied with the tip of your finger).
3. REPAIRING EYELETS: If the fabric is torn around the eyelets, glue on a narrow strip of unbleached muslin or leather under the eyelet and large enough to include a little of the area around the eyelet. Pierce holes through fabric at eyelet. (A leather punch may be a luxury, but it makes nice neat round holes!)

CUSTOMIZING NEW SHOES: If you are tired of the same old black or white leather shoes that are available commercially "customize" them by doing this:
4. COLOR NEW SHOES: Buy spray-on dye especially made for leather, available in many colors. Spray shoes the color desired (there might be enough dye left for your own shoes) and use narrow matching ribbons for ties and trim.
5. COVER NEW SHOES WITH FABRIC: If you would like to match the doll's dress, buy shoes of the correct length and do this:
   a. Carefully remove outer sole with a sharp knife. If the shoes need further fitting you may loosen the upper from the inner sole and cut to fit doll's foot. Replace inner sole by gluing with white glue.
   b. Cut fabric the same shape as the upper part of the shoe and about 1/4in (0.65cm) larger all around. Experiment until you have the right shape. Check some of the patterns in A, B and C for approximate shapes.
   c. Glue fabric to uppers, making sure that it lies flat and smooth.
   d. Starting at the center front, glue fabric to the sole gradually working toward the center back, pulling taut to eliminate wrinkles. Trim away any excess fabric, allowing for a 1/4in (0.65cm) overlap at CB. At CB apply glue and overlap. (If you prefer, the CB's may be sewn before applying to sole.) Turn top edge of fabric over the top edge of the shoe and glue for a neat finish. Re-shape outer sole if necessary and glue in place.

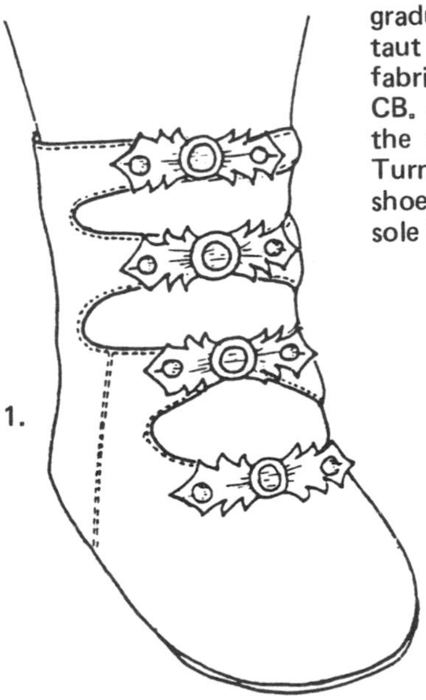

Illustration 104. View of shoe from pattern 11.

6. USING TRIM
   a. BRAID: Matching tiny braid will often add a nice touch around top of uppers, and possibly at the line where sole and upper meet.
   b. BUTTONS: If you need buttons, try making French knot buttons as shown in *Illustration 111,* as follows: Use Perlene or rather heavy embroidery thread. Bring needle and thread through fabric to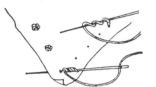

Illustration 111. French knot.

   right side. Wind thread around the needle from four to twelve times depending on the size of thread and size of the button required. Insert needle 1/16in (0.15cm) away from the thread and hold loops flat with one finger while drawing needle to wrong side. Secure.
7. OTHER TRIM: See RIBBON, Section 15, for ribbon trim rosettes and bows which can be used on shoes.

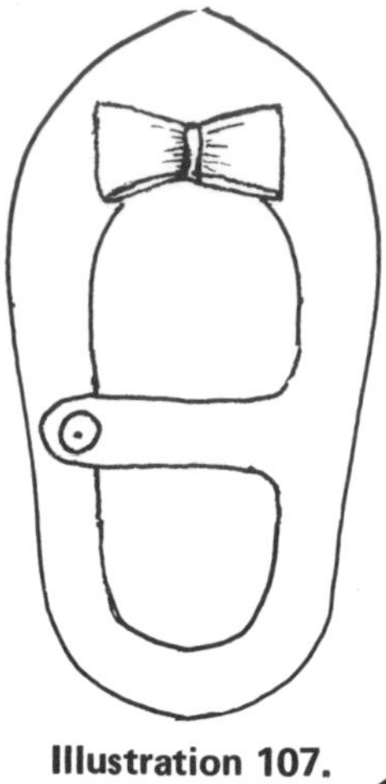

Illustration 107.

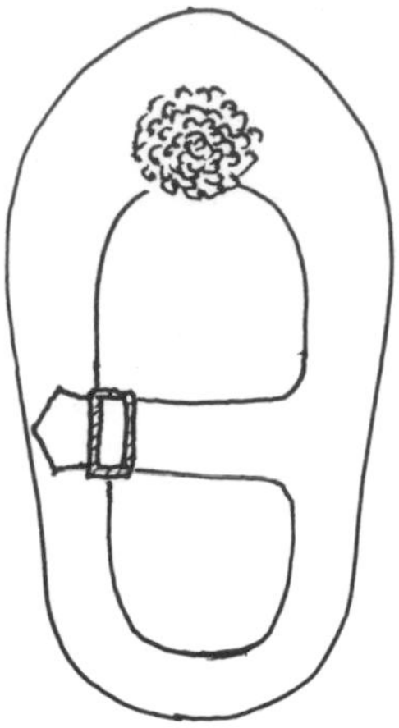

Illustration 108.

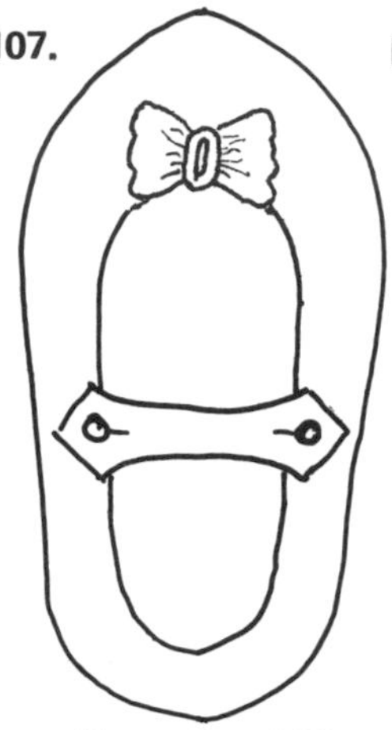

Illustration 109.

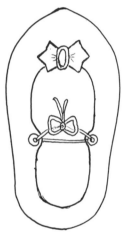

Illustration 105.

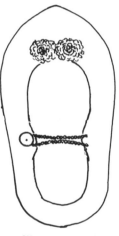

Illustration 106.

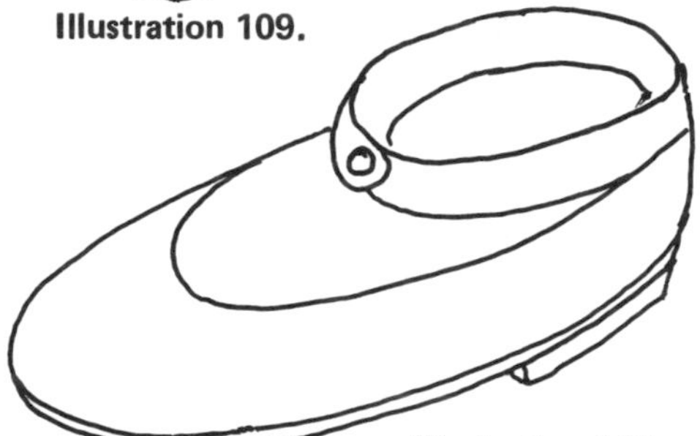

Illustration 110.

A LITTLE EXTRA HELP FOR WOULD-BE SHOEMAKERS

a. Be sure to trim seams where possible. The 1/4in (0.65cm) seam allowance is actually a little generous but until the costumer becomes more skilled in these techniques the seam allowance provides a slight margin for error (or correction).

b. When folding fabric or leather over the sole, note that the material can be squeezed or worked into a smaller space. On tiny shoes, the seam allowance may have to be smaller.

c. On both fabric and leather the upper can be finished with binding of ribbon or self-fabric, or with a tiny zigzag stitch with thread that matches the fabric.

d. Keep in mind that these patterns are not intended for a specific doll, so do fit the sole to your doll to insure ample room for the doll's feet . . . remember that socks or stockings use a little space and the shoes must be fit over them.

SECTION TWENTY
Bonnets

Little girls' bonnets have always been enchanting, more enchanting than practical if one were to judge from some of the elaborately lacy, be-ribboned and plumed creations which filled the fashion books of the 1880s and 1890s. On dolls, however, they add a note of charm and give the doll costumer justification for going "all out," allowing her imagination and her trimming hand unlimited liberty to create a masterpiece. Of course, this must be done under the restraint of fashions consistent with the period in which the doll is being dressed; but again, as one can see from some of the pictures, there were not many limits to be observed. In any case a bonnet or hat adds a note of charm to a doll outfit, and who knows - - perhaps satisfies the inner needs of ladies who no longer wear hats themselves.

Here are shown a few of the variations which characterized children's headwear, to give a few hints to doll costumers for bonnets appropriate to dresses of specific periods.

One note of caution. There seems to be a tendency when dressing dolls to put together any cute little combination of cardboard, ribbon and lace, ruffles and furbelows and label it a hat. However, we like to think that authenticity can be carried over to bonnets and hats, as well as in underwear and dresses. To that end we try to include an authentic antique hat style with most of our patterns. Sometimes these require the development of new techniques in the use of wire and buckram, but it is really worth the effort when one views the end results and realizes that these products represent reasonable facsimiles of the hats worn during the period in question. We have tried to keep these techniques as simple as possible for the novice.

So we hope that the dated illustrations taken from old *The Delineators* and shown here will provide limits within which the costumer can work, assured that her creations will be consistent with the rest of the costume. We also suggest referring to sections on ribbon, lace and bows in this book for many suggestions that will help in developing trim for hats and bonnets.

FIGURE A.—THE "PET."

Illustration 112. Bonnets and hats 1880 to 1890s.

111

SECTION TWENTY-ONE

... And Bows

Bows on bonnets, bows on frocks, single bows, or double bows .. as decorative trim, to tie on one's bonnet or adorn hats .. they look so simple yet often elude the home sewer who strives to get that casual or that tailored look. Made of self-fabric* as in dress sashes, bustles and cummerbunds, or ribbon used on bonnets and hats, the techniques are the same. Some of the following kinds of bows should be helpful to doll costumers.

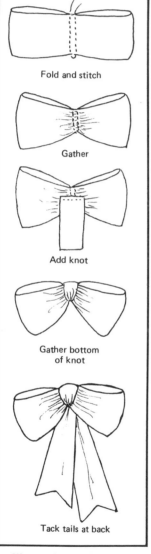

Illustration 113. Bow construction.

TAILORED BOW, with a soft finish suitable for dress fronts and backs, bonnets, hats and shoes.

a. BOW: Cut one rectangle a little more than twice the length of the bow desired. If self-fabric, hem both long edges. Fold ends to center, ends just touching. Hold in place with long basting threads; then run gathering stitches by hand along both cut edges and pull in gently to about half the width of the bow. This gathering could be replaced by a simple box pleat tacked in place, but in either case reduce the width to about one-half the original size.

b. KNOT: Cut a square of bias fabric long enough to go around the center of the bow with 1/2in (1.3cm) overlap (as for example, 2in [5.1cm] by 2in [5.1cm]). Stitch the two cut edges; turn inside out. Tack on bow as shown in *Illustration 113,* bringing end of knot around and overlap. Tack in place. Keep knot wide at top of bow and gather in a little at the bottom to simulate a tied bow. After completing the knot, curve both ends of the bow downward as shown in *Illustration 113* and tack.

c. "TAILS" for BOWS: Bow ends are most easily made using one long strip of fabric cut the same width as that of the bows and about the same length as the strip from which the bow was made. Hem long edges or finish to match bow, and cut the ends in a point, a V or at an angle as desired, or fringe. FOLD OFF-CENTER so that one tail will be slightly longer than the other and tack to back of knot. *Illustration 113.*

DOUBLE BOW, similar to tailored bow except that an additional loop gives it a more bouffant look.

a. Follow directions for first loop of tailored bow, but do not add knot.

b. Cut a rectangle slightly smaller than that of the first loop and proceed as with the first loop. Set second bow on top of the first, centering and tacking together. Apply knot as described for the tailored bow, curve and tack.

c. Add "tails" as shown for first bow.

EXAMPLE WITH MEASUREMENTS. This bow might be suitable for the back trim of an 18in (45.7cm) doll.

a. Cut rectangle 5in (12.7cm) by 14in (35.6cm). Hem and fold ends toward center as explained in tailored bow.

b. Knot; cut a square of fabric 2in (5.1cm) by 2in (5.1cm) and apply.

c. Tails - - cut a strip 5in (12.7cm) by 10in (25.4cm). Follow directions for TAILS.

BOWS OF DOUBLED FABRIC. Bows may be made from fabric doubled and sewn in a tube and turned inside out, thus eliminating the need for long tedious hemming. When cutting, double the width of the bow and add 1/2in (1.3cm) seam allowance; machine-stitch long raw edges together; turn inside out and press; then proceed as for the single bow. Follow the same procedure for the tails.

MORE BOWS. An interesting page of bows (shown here in *Illustration 114*) from *The Delineator* of 1886 shows a number of variations on tying bows. No instructions are given as they can easily be copied. Note that the fabrics from which the bows are made include flowered, striped and lace-edged.

*See: Ribbon, page 94, for directions on how to make your own self-fabric ribbon.

THE DELINEATOR.

Illustration 114. Bows from *The Delineator.*

SECTION TWENTY-TWO
Hints Of All Kinds

The following information is a grouping of suggestions for processes and methods which may facilitate your sewing or perhaps indicate little techniques with which you are unfamiliar. Since there are always new people entering the field of doll-costuming, persons with limited experience in any kind of sewing, or sewing for dolls specifically, we believe that this list is worthy of careful study.

The suggestions have been classified according to their specific areas, although there is occasional overlapping. In any case, searching through a great many ideas has, we hope, been somewhat simplified for you by our efforts to break them down into categories. These classifications are as follows:

FABRICS: cotton, silk, cutting ruffles, felt, fabrics with naps, raveling, lace.

PATTERNS: cutting, correction, notches, marking, cutting linings.

SEWING: cutting, fabric grain, using silk thread, placing gathers, stitches, seams, closures, hems.

PRESSING: use of brown paper, organdy, paint brushes, ribbons and lace.

NEEDLES: kind of machine, kind of hand, numbering, fabric use.

THREAD: types, size, cutting, double thread.

STITCH SIZE: for sewing machines.

DYEING: silk, buttons, lace, fabrics, drying, pressing.

TRIM: selvages, soutache braid.

STOCKINGS: making, holding up.

GLUING: fabrics, attaching wigs.

WIGS: when dressing dolls, dowels for curlers, mohair.

HANDY HINTS FOR HOME USERS

FABRICS: Cotton. If cotton is very soft, add body by pressing with spray starch. The slight stiffness obtained will make sewing on the fabric easier, and the stiffness will disappear shortly.

FABRICS: Storage . . . silks should be refolded frequently while being stored to prevent threads creasing and breaking. Folding over tissue paper or rolling in tissue paper will protect silks.

FABRICS: Silk. If silk is stiff, experiment with a small piece and some fabric softener. Pure silk should be washable, so fabric softener can be used to remove some of the stiffness.

FABRICS: Soft ruffles. For soft-falling ruffles or for soft-falling gathered skirts try using fabrics *lengthwise* instead of crosswise. Put a few inches of gathering threads in material both lengthwise and crosswise to determine which hangs softly in small folds. Check design and grain of fabric first to be sure that skirt treated in this manner does not look different from the rest of the dress. Some fabrics look quite different on the cross grain of the fabric, in which case the complete garment should be cut either lengthwise or crosswise of grain.

FABRIC needed for pleating and gathering: When doing knife pleating, for a finished length of pleating, three times that length of material will be required. For pleats farther apart, somewhat less material will be required, but it is best to plan on a little more than the measurement indicates, as lapping will take a few extra pleats. For gathering, almost the same proportions (three to one) will be needed, although in the case of gathers, obviously a smaller amount of material can be adjusted to the band or dress to which the gathering will be attached. NOTE: THIS DOES NOT APPLY WHEN CARTRIDGE PLEATING IS BEING USED.

FABRICS: Fabrics with naps. Be sure to hand baste before machine-stitching and always sew in the direction of the nap so that the pieces will not "travel."

FABRICS: Fabrics with naps. Pressing. Napped fabrics should be steamed with the iron hovering over the fabric but never touching it; or place over a "needleboard." This is a flat pressing surface of short nails placed very close together. Fabric is placed NAP side down to avoid crushing. These are available in most fabric stores.

FABRICS: Raveling. If the dress material ravels easily, zigzag around edge of dress and lining pieces *separately* and press before combining them.

FABRICS: Raveling. A very light layer of glue on the edge before sewing will discourage raveling. Do the gluing with discretion, as you cannot sew through glue easily.

FABRICS: Lace. Lace may be shaped into a curve by the method shown for RIBBON. With a steam iron, press the scalloped edge of lace in a swirling motion while holding the straight edge taut. This will give a pleasant slight fullness to lace which is to be sewn on straight with no gathers.

FABRICS: Lace. When working with very fragile lace, face with tulle or English net, using tiny stitches overall, with ecru lingerie thread. Stitches and tulle will be almost invisible but will strengthen the lace enough so that you can sew it.

FABRIC: Lace. To find the correct or right side is often difficult, but often floral designs are outlined in a fine thread which can be detected with a magnifying glass, by rubbing fingers over the lace to detect roughness, or by examining the wrong side which will have a completely smooth look.

FABRICS: Lace. For storing lace, wrap in acid-free tissue paper or in an acid-free box available from a museum supply house. The reason for this is that ordinary paper yellows lace. If the boxes are not available, a clean white cotton sheet is a good substitute.

FABRICS: Felt. Wash in hot water and run through a hot dryer, to obtain an appearance surprisingly like real leather.

FABRICS: Fabrics with naps. All pattern pieces must be cut in the same direction on napped fabrics. Velvet, velveteen and panne should be used with nap running UP, to get full benefit of color. You will have to judge which you prefer. We have found that in some pale colors, we prefer the nap running down.

PATTERNS: Cutting. When cutting old garments, be sure to establish straight grain of fabric before placing patterns.

PATTERNS: Basic. On a basic pattern only one side of the corrected pattern need be used for the final adjustment and completion of a final form to be used for cutting.

PATTERNS: Notches. Do not cut into fabric where notches are indicated. Either cut outward or mark. On small garments or on very sheer fabrics you might otherwise cut too close to the seam line.

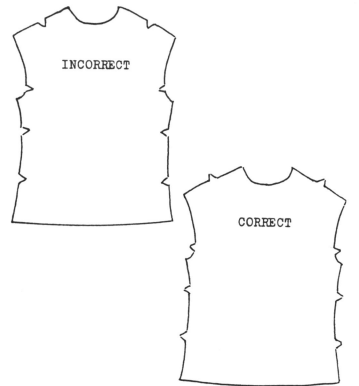

Illustration 115. Figure showing correct placement of notches on sheer material.

PATTERNS: Notches. In all commercial patterns and in Ulseth-Shannon patterns as well, one notch in the armseye and on the sleeve always indicates the front, two notches the back of the garment.

PATTERNS: Notches. In many antique garments the sleeve seam is placed in the back of the armseye and NOT at the underarm seam as in modern clothes. This point is obvious when working with a coat sleeve that has two seams, but confusing with the one-seam sleeve.

PATTERNS: Marking. When cutting patterns, use a chalk pencil . . . marks can be washed off fabric following manufacturer's directions.

PATTERNS: Cutting linings . . . made easier! To eliminate precise cutting twice for one garment, cut the lining pieces as perfectly as possible. Lay these lining pieces on the silk or other dress fabric. Pin and baste around edges. THEN cut top fabric around the lining edges. Be careful to maintain straight of fabric when placing lining pieces on top fabric. With this method, lining and top fabric are already joined and can be treated as one piece.

SEWING: Place a folded turkish towel on your lap for convenience when doing hand sewing. It will hold pins and needles, sewing will not slip and slide, and work can be anchored to the towel with a pin.

SEWING: Cutting. It is of utmost importance to observe and follow instructions for cutting along straight grain of fabric. Even a slight error will result in "skewing" or failure of garment to hang straight from shoulder or waistband (unless deliberately cut on bias). One other exception . . . on small garments with gathered skirts, the skirt may hang more softly if made on lengthwise grain instead of cross grain of fabric (see FABRIC: Soft ruffles).

TO DETERMINE CORRECT GRAIN of fabric lengthwise and crosswise:

LENGTHWISE: Threads parallel to selvage will show lengthwise grain. Some fabrics can be torn lengthwise, thus establishing grain line.

CROSSWISE:
1. Cut on a 90 degree angle from selvage for cross-grain, or clip selvage and tear from selvage to selvage.
2. Snip selvage and gently pull one thread. Fabric will gather slightly along pulled thread. Cut here for crosswise grain.

SEWING: Sewing with silk thread. Silk threads drawn from the edge of the fabric can be used as sewing thread in the garment for hand sewing on any fine hemming . . . invisible! Use double thread for more strength.

SEWING: Sewing with silk thread. Silk thread can be used for basting and any fine work. When pressed, it should not leave any marks on the fabric.

SEWING: Placement of gathering stitches. When placing gather stitches, stitch one row 3/8in (0.9cm) from edge of garment, a second 1/8in (0.31cm) from edge of garment using machine foot as a guide. Pull to desired size, pin in place and machine-stitch *between* the two gathering rows. After finishing the work, the exposed row of gathers can be removed easily.

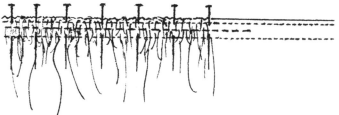

Illustration 116. Figure showing correct placement of gathering stitches.

SEWING: Gathering stitches. Gathers may be distributed evenly by running a heavy needle or a hat pin back and forth between the two rows of stitching.

SEWING: Seams. If a garment calls for 1/8in (0.31cm) seams, which are difficult to sew on sheer fabrics, cut garments larger (by 1/8in [0.31cm]) and mark the original sewing lines; sew on the line and then trim to 1/8in (0.31cm) after sewing. If seam allowance required is 1/4in (0.65cm), cut 3/8in (0.9cm) and trim after sewing.

SEWING: Seams. When working with sheer fabrics, place tissue paper under seam before machine-stitching is done to provide body and prevent fabric from getting caught in feed-dogs. When finished, tear tissue paper away from stitching.

SEWING: Closures. On dress closures which require tight fitting, reverse hooks and eyes so that alternately the hook will be on one side of the closure, and the next on the other side. The eye would then, of course, be reversed to match hooks. This method is often found on ladies' antique garments, particularly on bodices where there was much strain. When applied in this manner it is easy to see how the counter-balancing of the hooks prevents the garment from popping open.

SEWING: Tiny hems. When a tiny hem is necessary such as around armseyes on slips, down front openings of underwear, and on bias material, try this: machine-stitch with short stitch a short distance from edge of opening, perhaps 1/8in (0.31cm) or even 1/16in (0.15cm). Turn and press on stitching line to form first fold. Fold again and hem by hand. The stitching will give you a firm hold on the fabric and prevent raveling.

PRESSING: Lace and ribbon . . . a repeat, but so important. Lace and ribbon may be curved to conform to circular patterns or to allow lace to stand out a little from garment when gathers are not being used. Press to shape with iron by pressing in a swirling motion the outside of the lace while holding the inner edge taut.

PRESSING: Using brown paper. Place a strip of brown paper under seam allowances to avoid an imprint when pressing.

PRESSING: Using organdy. A square of cotton organdy makes an excellent transparent pressing cloth.

PRESSING: Using a paint brush! A small paint brush is handy for moistening areas to be pressed.

PRESSING: Lace and ribbon . . . a repeat! Ribbon, lace, tape or ribbon to be attached to a curved edge can be blocked to match the curve. Trace the curve of the pattern on the ironing board with chalk. Pin ribbon to curve. Steam press, keeping iron parallel with outer edge. To ease and shrink fullness at inner edge, while stretching outer edge, work iron inward, swirling toward inner edge. (See *Illustration 118*.)

NEEDLES: What size should you use? Use fine needles for fine sewing. Use No. 8 for hems and hand finishing, and No. 9 for basting, putting in sleeves and other general uses. See chart on page 116.

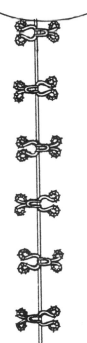

Illustration 117. Figure showing placement of hooks and eyes.

Note hooks and eyes positioned alternately on each side of opening.

THREAD: Kinds available. Look for Coats DUAL DUTY LINGERIE THREAD which comes on small spools and is equivalent to cotton No. 90 or No. 100, but is much stronger with a certain amount of "stretch" that reduces breakage. The ecru color blends in almost invisibly with light colors, but many colors are available.

THREAD: Double thread. When using double thread, knot ends singly and there will be less snarling as you start to work.

THREAD: Cutting thread. Cut thread at an angle; it will slip into the needle eye more easily . . you will not see the difference but "the needle knows."

STITCH LENGTH: Lengths for various purposes. Sewing machines have levers which can be used to adjust the length of the stitch, giving the number of stitches per inch. This guide may help you:

REGULAR STITCH: 12 to 15 per inch. Use for all general sewing but keep in mind that the shorter stitches will look better on small garments, and were, in fact, common on antique garments as you know if you have ever tried to remove lace from one. Use No. 12 for staystitching, except as noted below.

REINFORCE: Use 20 per inch, to strengthen corners, for use around curves to prevent stretching, as a base for handsewn buttonholes, etc.

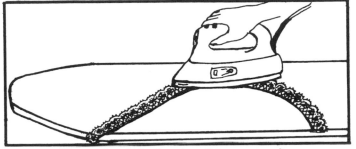

Illustration 118. Pressing ribbon or lace in a curve.

MACHINE BASTING AND GATHERING: Machine basting should be done with a long stitch, six or seven per inch, thus enabling you to remove the basting easily, and, of course, of fabrics of medium weight or heavy weight, to make the gathering possible. Note that on sheer fabrics of cotton or silk, a shorter stitch (12 per inch) can be used satisfactorily for gathering, and will, in fact, produce a much finer shirring than the larger stitch.

CHART: THREAD	Hand Needles	Machine Needles	Thread Size
Fabric Weight and Examples			
VERY SHEER: Batiste, chiffon, fine lace, organdy, net.	10	9	Cotton 90-100 or Polyester Lingerie
LIGHT: Dimity, dotted swiss, lawn, sheer crepe, voile, silk.	9	9-11	As above
MEDIUM: Broadcloth, gingham, taffeta, satin, wools, chintz, linen, flannel.	7-9	11-14	Cotton 50-60 or Polyester Regular
MEDIUM-HEAVY: Velveteen, terry, tweeds, drapery fabrics, twill.	6-7	14-16	Cotton 40 or Polyester Regular

Illustration 119.

NEEDLES: Hand needle size. Hand needles are numbered from 1 (the coarsest) to 10 (the finest). Consult chart for ideal use on various fabrics.

NEEDLES: Machine needle size. Machine needles are numbered from 9 (the finest) to 18 (the coarsest) for home sewing. Naturally for commercial purposes they come much larger. Consult chart for ideal use on various fabrics.

HAND NEEDLE GUIDE		
Type	Sizes	Uses
Milliners	3-10	Long needles for basting.
Sharps	10	For general sewing on filmy material such as voile, chiffon, net, jersey, crepe and silk.
Sharps	9	General sewing on sheer materials such as lawns, tricots, velvets and satins.
Sharps	8	General sewing on lightweight materials such as ginghams, flannel, jersey, crepe, etc.
Sharps	6	General sewing on medium weight such as corduroy, crash, muslin and other cottons.

Illustration 120.

NEEDLES: This chart shows suggested size of hand needles, for working on various types and weights of fabrics.

DYEING: Silk. Silk is a remarkably hardy fabric. It can be dyed with RIT coloring to freshen the color of old faded silks, or white and other light colors can be dyed almost any color you wish. If you decide to dye a length of silk, you might consider dyeing at the same time a length of cotton to match for lining or hat, cotton lace for trim or ribbon for a bonnet or sash. Even pearl buttons can be tinted. (See DYEING: Buttons.)

DYEING: Buttons. Pearl or plastic buttons may be immersed in dye bath for a few hours. They will not actually change color but will take on a "tinge" that allows them to blend with a fabric. This can be done on the stove . . simmer a few minutes in the dye bath.

DYEING: Lace. Colored lace was available as early as 1880. When a certain color of lace is required to match or contrast with a fabric, use RIT dyes and experiment with dyes and white cotton lace. Boiling is never necessary. Just dip until desired color is obtained. Remember that material is darker when wet, so iron a small sample completely dry to determine the actual color of the finished fabric.

DYEING: Lace. For narrow lace use an INSTANT coffee solution rather than tea. Let lace get quite dark, as much of the color will wash out leaving lace a lovely soft ecru.

DYEING: Fabrics. If you want to tone down a very bright new-looking material, dip it in a light solution of tan, ecru or brown dye. Experiment first with a trial bit for correct color, and iron *dry* before making a decision about the suitability of the new color.

DYEING: Drying. Drying small pieces of lace and ribbon may be facilitated by use of a small aluminum screen used as a drying rack.

DYEING: Pressing. A tinted fabric should be pressed while it is still damp. The heat helps to *set* the color.

DYEING: Pressing. Color intensity increases if soft water is used. To make hard water more effective, add a thimbleful of water softener to each quart of water

in the dye bath. (Note: Who among us home sewers does not have a thimble?)

TRIM: In antique clothes. In antique clothes it has been noted that most trim was APPLIED . . sometimes layer upon layer . . . so a basic dress can be made and "fancied up" as one wishes.

TRIM: Selvages. Watch for interesting selvages on fabrics. On close inspection some are found to be decorative (even woven in two or more colors) providing perfect trim edge with perfect color match. SHRINK before using.

TRIM: Braid. To finish a narrow braid such as soutache, pierce a hole in fabric, being careful not to break threads in the garment. Carefully force the ends of braid through the hole and hand tack on the under side.

TRIM: A beautiful little braid can be made by combining several strands of six-strand embroidery thread of different colors and braid together. Tack to dress when color contrast is indicated.

STOCKINGS: Holding them up. Use stockings long enough to cover legs up to torso. Put large gathering stitch around stocking and pull over the top of the leg and secure.

STOCKINGS: Holding them up. If the foregoing is not suitable for the type of doll on which you are working, suspenders may be made, with a narrow ribbon or tape tied around the waist to which are attached ribbons or tape long enough to reach the tops of the stockings. They may be pinned to the ribbons with tiny safety pins, or if the stockings are sturdy enough, snap fasteners can be sewn to ribbons and stockings and snapped together.

STOCKINGS: Make them yourself. Our one concession to modern fabrics when dressing antique dolls is the use of polyester panty hose or stockings with a fine mesh or flowered mesh design. Many of the older panty hose come in off-white colors with lovely mesh designs. These may be cut to the correct size, allowing for the amount of stretch in the fabric, and zigzagged with a close narrow stitch . . . and your doll has her own non-sag hose made to order.

GLUING: How to apply. Apply white glue from applicator in little beads around area to be glued. Spread evenly with finger, or better yet, with a corsage pin or a hat pin; slide it along beads of glue and spread evenly.

GLUING: For fabrics. When gluing two pieces of fabric together with white glue, apply a light layer of glue to both pieces, let set for a minute or two; then press together.

GLUING: Attaching wigs. Use a light layer of WHITE glue to hold wig in place. Since white glue is water-soluble, in the event that it is necessary to remove the wig, loosen the glue with a little water on a toothpick and lift wig off.

WIGS: When old wigs need to be re-curled, after shampooing use wooden dowels. Purchase at a hardware store 1/2in (1.3cm) dowels, and 1/4in (0.65cm) dowels. Cut the larger size about 4in (10.2cm) in length, and with a saw make a slot about 1/16in (0.15cm) deep at each end for holding a rubber band. Roll hair on the dowel, and hold in place with rubber band that is run through the slot at each end of the curler. The dowels slide out easily after the hair is dry.

WIGS: Curling. Take a tip from your beauty operator and use squares of paper at the ends of the hair before rolling to keep them in place.

WIGS: Mohair. Mohair may be set (CAREFULLY) either on dowels as indicated above, or curled around the finger and held in place with clips until dry.

SECTION TWENTY-THREE
Glossary Of Terms For Antique Clothing

People interested in dolls, and consequently in styles and fabrics used in fashions of the 19th and early 20th century, frequently are confronted with words not now part of our vocabulary. We have included two lists of definitions. One concerns terms relating to old styles and fashions which are encountered in books and fashion magazines of the 1880s and 1890s as well as a few simple sewing terms. While this list is by no means inclusive, it should serve as a handy reference for those terms most often used to describe styles of the period mentioned.

The second list of definitions includes fabrics only. Many of these fabrics have been in common use for decades, but this fairly inclusive list should provide a convenient reference when they are found in old magazines, catalogs and books.

GLOSSARY

APPLIQUE: the process of cutting out designs of contrasting fabrics and embroidering or sewing them onto a garment for decorative purposes.

ARMSEYE: the opening in a bodice or dress top for inserting a sleeve.

BASQUE: a woman's blouse made with a tight-fitting waist and with or without a short skirt or peplum attached.

BERTHA: a wide collar worn around a neckline, often made of lace, sometimes of matching or contrasting material.

BRETELLE: suspender-like, shaped bands worn over shoulders and attached in back and front to a waistband; often used to help support a skirt, and sometimes applied as trim.

CHATELAINE: an ornamental hook, clasp, or brooch worn at a woman's waist having a chain (or ribbon or string) attached for keys, trinkets, purse, watch or sewing needs.

CHEMISETTE: a vest or dickey, generally sleeveless, and made of fine cotton and lace or net; used primarily to fill a low neckline.

CLOSURE: opening of any garment which makes it possible to put garment on more easily.

COMBINATION: a top combined with drawers to form a one-piece undergarment. Sometimes referred to as a chemise-drawers.

CUIR: French word for leather.

CULOTTE: baby drawers (as opposed to our present use of the word).

CUMMERBUND: a broad pleated sash worn on a dress, usually with a dropped waistline.

DROPPED FLY: a flap on the front of boys' or men's pants popular up to the 1840s when a standard front fly replaced it for general use.

DUST RUFFLE: a ruffle, usually pleated in pleats from 1/4in (0.65cm) to 1in (2.5cm) of tarlatan edged with lace. This was placed under the hem of children's dresses for stiffening under the skirt, or on floor-length dresses around hemline to "pick up the dust," hence the word "dust ruffle." This also served to hold the skirt out and to stiffen it.

FICHU: A kind of ornamental three-cornered cape, usually of lace, muslin, or silk, worn by women as a covering for the shoulders.

FLOCKING: decorative trim on fabrics consisting of tiny dots either woven in or later applied in the manufacturing process.

FLOUNCE: deep gathered or pleated ruffles.

FLUTER: a small (about 8in [20.3cm] by 8in [20.3cm] by 10in [25.4cm]) pressing machine with two hollow parallel bars indented on the outside with longitudinal ridges that meshed when turned with a handle. These were heated by means of iron rods heated on a stove and inserted into the hollow cores of the brass rollers. Fabrics were run slowly between the rollers and pressed into the long narrow pattern or ridges on the rollers.

GARNITURE: decorative trim of all kinds.

GAUGING; See PLEATING, CARTRIDGE

GIMP: an ornamental flat braid or round cord used as trimming.

GODET: a segment of cloth wider at the bottom than at the top and used as an inset to produce fullness or for widening, such as in a skirt. (Also: Gore)

GUIMPE: a blouse with either long or short sleeves worn under open-neck dresses.

KILT: a small boy's skirted garment sometimes worn over short tight or bloused pants . . . or without. Usually they were worn by boys from two to five years of age. The word also designates a girl's pleated skirt.

KNICKERS: a development from women's straight leg drawers to a type gathered on a band below the knees with a ruffle of embroidered edging. Boys aged five to fourteen also wore "knickers" from around 1910 to the 1930s (no lace, of course!).

MERCERIZING: an important preparatory process for cotton fabrics or linen. Mercerizing causes the flat twisted ribbon-like cotton fiber to swell into a round shape and to contract in length. The fiber becomes much more lustrous and the strength is increased by 20 percent (hence the advantage of mercerized thread for hand- and machine-sewing).

MILLINERS WIRE: a type of cotton-wrapped wire packaged in rolls, black and white, and in several weights, used in making ladies' hat frames and children's hats and bonnets.

PALETOT: a cloak, usually long, with one or more capes.

PANTALETTE: fancy laced and ruffled legs sewn on a band or elastic and worn from knee to ankle under full skirts.

PASSEMENTERIE: a fancy edging or trimming made of braid, cord, gimp, beading or metallic thread in various combinations.

PASTEBOARD: an old name for cardboard.

PELERINE: a full-length cloak or coat, often fur trimmed or fur lined.

PELISSE: a long cloak for outdoor wear, sometimes fur lined.

PLASTRON: a trimming like a dickey worn on the front of a woman's dress.

PLEATING:
1. BOX PLEATING . . . a system of pleating two edges together, skipping a space and bringing two more folded edges together.

2. CARTRIDGE PLEATING . . . a method of pleating great widths of material to be gathered into a small space as, for example, when dressing a china doll with a tiny waist when you want a bouffant skirt. See Section EIGHT. (Also referred to as ORGAN PLEATING or GAUGING.)

3. KNIFE PLEATING . . . ordinary pleats of any size with firmly pressed folds going in the same direction.

4. UNPRESSED PLEATS . . . pleats sewn in at the top but allowed to hang free with no pressing or crease marks.

POLONAISE: dress top hanging below the waist and often draped in back.

RIBBON WIRE: a narrow (1/4in [0.65cm] to 1/2in [1.3cm]) stiff fabric with fine wire molded into each edge.

RUCHE OR RUCHING: a narrow band of net, lace or fine thin fabric, set in pleats or gathers, applied to trim a dress, particularly at necklines and wrists.

SHIFT: another name for chemise.

SLEEVES:

BISHOP SLEEVE: wide, full sleeve gathered at wrists.

COAT SLEEVE: a straight sleeve with a slight curve at the elbow, or often made in two sections as for suits or tailored garments.

PAGODA SLEEVE: bell-shaped sleeve (about seven-eights length) with sheer gathered undersleeve.

UNDERSLEEVE: sheer partial sleeve, usually quite full, worn under pagoda sleeves . . . attached on a band to fit over the elbow, and gathered at wrists.

WARP: threads on a loom used to form the length of the fabric.

WOOF: (also FILLING OR WEFT) . . . threads on a loom used to form the width of the fabric.

SECTION TWENTY-FOUR
Glossary Of Fabrics

ALPACA (mohair): a shiny, stiff, wiry cloth made of Angora goat hair and with either cotton, wool or silk filling.

ALBATROSS: a lightweight woolen fabric in which the plain weave has been varied to produce a crepe effect. It is usually soft, but has more body than challis.

ARMURE: silk or woolen material whose weave resembles chained armor.

BALBRIGGAN: formerly denoted the highest grade of fine knit underwear, but now applied to any kind of underwear made of Egyptian cotton.

BATISTE: a semi-sheer lightweight cotton fabric with a soft silky feel and a silky appearance, distinguished from nainsook by its finer construction and finish.

BENGALINE: a heavy corded silk fabric with a silk warp and a cotton or worsted filling.

BOBBINET: see NET.

BOMBAZINE: a fine twilled fabric of silk and worsted or cotton, often dyed black and used for mourning.

BUCKRAM: a stiff, coarse, inexpensive cotton cloth heavily sized, used for the linings and frames of hats.

CALICO: an inexpensive cotton fabric with a plain weave and usually a printed pattern. It is rather coarse, heavily sized, and has a slightly glazed finish.

CAMBRIC: a closely woven, rather stiff cotton fabric with a slightly glossy surface. It was often used for underwear, corset-covers, combinations, drawers and chemises.

CASHMERE: a soft, lightweight, smooth material in a twill weave, made either of wool or with a cotton or silk warp, and usually found in plain colors. It was used for babies' sacques and coats and children's fall and winter dresses.

CHALLIS (wool): a lightweight woolen fabric in a plain weave or with a small printed design. It was used for dresses and kimonos.

CHALLIS (cotton): a medium weight cotton fabric finished to resemble wool challis. It usually has a printed pattern and is used when an inexpensive fabric is desired.

CHAMBRAY: a cotton material, always made with a colored warp and a white filling, which produces a grayed effect. It was often used for children's dresses and rompers, women's dresses and other wear.

CHINA SILK: a thin plain silk with a slight luster. It is similar to "Japanese" silk and to "Habutai" and all are used for lining baby dresses and ladies' waists and for making baby dresses.

COUTIL: a heavy cotton cloth used for making corsets with herringbone weave and sleek smooth appearance.

CRASH: a term loosely applied to any cotton or linen fabric which is constructed from coarse yarns in a plain loose weave. Better qualities were used for suits, separate skirts and toweling.

CRINOLINE: a coarse, medium weight cotton cloth, heavily sized, more closely woven than buckram and not quite so stiff.

DAMASSE SILK: a kind of brocaded silk material.

DIMITY: a very fine, sheer cotton fabric recognized by small cords or groups of small cords arranged in stripes or cross-bars. (Cross-bar dimity is called JACONET.)

DRAP D'ETE: lightweight cottons suitable for summer wear.

DUVETYN: a soft, short napped fabric with a twill weave, made of cotton, wool, rayon or silk.

FAILLE: a ribbed silk fabric recognized by its flat cord surface, the heavy filling cords being not so rounded as those in poplin and grosgrain, and inconspicuous. In effect, faille resembles taffeta, having about the same amount of stiffness.

FOULARD: a lightweight silk made with a plain twill or satin weave. It has a rich luster on the right side and usually comes in a printed pattern although it can be bought in plain colors. It feels light, firm, supple and slippery.

GALLOON: a narrow band or braid used as trimming and commonly made of lace, metallic thread embroidery.

GEORGETTE: a very thin sheer silk, with a crepe finish.

GINGHAM: a medium weight cotton material which comes in stripes, plaid and plain colors. Finer grades have a higher thread count (number of warp and woof threads used in the weaving process).

GRENADINE: a cloth of very open texture constructed in the gauze weave; usually made of silk and worsted. It often has fancy stripes of different weaves.

GROS DE LONDRES: a lightweight silk fabric of about the same texture as taffeta, but having narrow cords alternating with wider ones. The cords are flat and not so apparent as in a poplin or grosgrain. Often the warp and filling are of different colors, giving a changeable effect.

GROSGRAIN: an all-silk fabric with cords that are uniform in size, especially found in ribbon.

HABUTAI: (wash or tub silk) . . a lightweight Japanese silk very closely constructed in a plain weave. It has more body, is firmer, heavier and duller than CHINA SILK.

HENRIETTA: a fine woolen cloth.

JACONET: (See DIMITY.)

LAWN: a thin, lightweight rather stiff cotton in plain weave.

LININGS: (See BUCKRAM, CRINOLINE, TARLATAN) (Innerlinings, for dust ruffles and stiffening.)

LINSEY-WOOLSEY: a wool and linen fabric, with linen threads forming the warp and cotton or wool forming the woof or filler.

MALINE: (See NET.)

MASALIA: a trade name for a very fine underwear material which is heavier and has more body than nainsook.

MERINO: a soft lightweight fabric made originally of fine wool. ALSO, a type of fine wool and cotton yarn used for knitting underwear and hosiery.

MOIRE: usually a corded silk or silk-and-cotton fabric with a watered effect produced by pressing.

MOUSSELINE DE SOIE (SILK MUSLIN): a thin silk-and-cotton fabric with very little body, often having large printed patterns in soft colors.

MULL: one of the sheerest cotton fabrics made, mercerized with no dressing, hence soft; crushes quickly and needs frequent pressing.

MUSLIN: a term applied to any plain-woven fabric of close construction, ranging from the very finest grades of underwear material to the coarsest sheeting.

NAINSOOK: a thin lightweight cotton with a plain weave and little or no dressing; sometimes mercerized; not so thin and sheer as batiste.

NET:
1. BOBBINET: a cotton net, the threads so inter-woven that they form octagonal meshes, thus making a thin, transparent but strong fabric.
2. ENGLISH NET: a finely meshed fabric made of cotton; the background fabric of many types of lace.
3. MALINE: a fine silk or cotton hexagonal mesh netting, heavily sized, especially desirable for veilings and scarves.
4. POINT D'ESPRIT: a fine cotton net with small square spots at close and regular intervals. It is dainty, durable, and almost transparent.
5. TULLE: a silk net, very delicate and fragile, used for evening dresses, scarves and trimmings.

NUN'S VAILING: a lightweight wool fabric made with a plain weave in plain colors; similar to wool batiste.

ORGANDY: a sheer, stiff, very lightweight cotton, quite transparent and not durable.

PEAU DE SOIE: a heavy silk with a fine grainy surface produced by tiny cords, enduring and serviceable.

PERCALE: a cotton fabric with a plain weave, usually recognized by its firm construction, its smooth dull finish and its printed pattern, although it also comes in plain colors.

PINA CLOTH: a very sheer lustrous cloth with a plain weave made from the fibers of the pineapple. It is strong, durable and attractive, but stiff and unyielding.

PONGEE: a medium weight silk fabric in plain weave distinguished by its irregular threads. It is made of wild silk, and hence not so regular, fine, nor beautiful as fabrics made from cultivated silk.

POPLIN: a fine-ribbed material found in silk, wool, cotton, cotton-and-silk, silk-and-wool and wool-and-cotton. Its warp yarns are so fine and numerous as to cover completely the coarser filling yarns, thus producing fine ribs across the cloth.

RAMIE: a cloth similar to linen, made of ramie fiber which is strong, fine and durable.

SATEEN: a heavy mercerized cotton fabric with a sateen weave, attractive and durable but not so beautiful nor so soft as silk.

SATIN: a lustrous silk material in a satin weave. Satin is always made in the satin or a variation of the satin weave, but it may be finished with either a crepe or a plain back.

SCRIM: a cotton fabric made of heavy yarns in an open, plain weave, strong, durable, semitransparent, easily laundered.

SHANTUNG: silk similar to pongee; this is more irregular in weave.

SILK BROADCLOTH: a firm, lightweight silk fabric with a dull finish distinguished by its characteristic thick and heavy feel without the slipperiness of many silks.

SURAH: a soft, but stout silk, with a twill weave, usually with a dull surface although satin surah has a rather high luster.

SWISS (muslin): a fine thin cotton fabric rather loosely woven and having a great deal of stiffening. It differs from lawn in being more sheer, more loosely woven and stiffer.

SWISS (dotted): Swiss muslin with dots of heavier yarn at regular intervals. In good grades the dots are woven in and tied so that they will not wash out.

TAFFETA: a plain closely woven, rather stiff silk fabric with a dull luster. Chiffon taffeta is a more soft and pliable fabric. Many taffetas are heavily weighted and do not stand the test of time. (Many grades of taffeta are available in rayon but are usually unsatisfactory because of a bright sheen; they are too stiff to drape well, and do not wear well. They are not recommended for doll clothes.)

TARLATAN: a very loosely constructed cotton cloth, heavily sized, used most extensively for fancy dress costumes and decorative purposes and for ladies' petticoats and dust ruffles.

VELVET: a pile fabric with the pile usually cut close. Velvets are usually identified further by the kind of backing that is used, thus there are:
1. VELVETEEN with cotton backing and cotton pile.
2. COTTON-BACKED VELVET, a cotton backing with silk pile.
3. SILK-BACKED VELVET with silk pile and silk backing.
4. UPHOLSTERY VELVET with wool, mohair or linen backing.
5. LYONS VELVET with a cotton or silk back and with very close and firm backing.
6. CHIFFON VELVET, an all-silk velvet so woven that the pile is in very narrow stripes so fine that they are not noticeable unless examined closely.
7. PANNE VELVET, a cotton or silk-backed fabric, with pile longer than that of ordinary velvet, pressed to give a smooth, shiny effect.

VICUNA: a fabric made from the fleece of a vicuna (a llama-like animal of the central Andes in South America).

VIGNONE: an all-wool cloth, twilled in neutral colors, originally of Spanish wool.

VOILE: made in cotton, silk and wool, a fabric made of fine, hard-twisted yarns with a plain weave and open mesh.

WORSTED: while woolens and worsteds are both made of wool, there is a difference in the length of the fiber, weave and finish. Woolen yarns have short fibers, tend to be soft and fuzzy. Worsted yarns are longer, tend to be smooth and strong.

ZEPHYR: a fine, lightweight woolen fabric.
OR
light, fine gingham, thin and silky.

ZIBELINE: a thick lustrous soft fabric of wool and other animal hair such as mohair, having a silky nap.

SECTION TWENTY-FIVE
Identification Of Fabrics

In the past few years polyester fabrics have almost replaced the old, traditional fabrics of silk, linen, wool and untreated cotton. Since many fabrics contain combinations of these fibers with polyesters, it is almost impossible to distinguish between pure natural fabrics and those containing synthetics. For some home sewers, however, it is important to be able to recognize the difference since they want to work with those fabrics common to the period in which their dolls were manufactured. Perhaps a garmant has been picked up in a garage sale, the idenfitication of which is difficult, or an old garment from someone's attic may or may not be pure silk. There are many kinds of tests which can be used to determine fiber content but for our purpose only a few are important and practical. These may not be infallible but will at least give some hint as to probable identification. Since our interest is primarily in natural fabrics, only these have been included with two exceptions, rayon and acetate. Tests for these are shown in order to give some basis for comparison with the results expected for pure fabrics.

FEEL TEST:

One of the essential methods of identifying fabrics is through a process in which most fabric shoppers engage almost without realizing its significance. They pick up a fabric and feel it to evaluate the weight, texture, softness or wiriness. They think about such qualities as stretch, laundering, shape-holding capacity and draping capacity. All these factors are important in dressing dolls since it is essential to avoid bulk, to use fabrics which are soft enough to hang well, and in some cases have a desirable, soft luster.

SO: First feel the cloth in which you are interested, keeping these points in mind:

COTTON: is cool to the touch and feels soft and inelastic.

LINEN: is cold and smooth and has a leathery feel.

WOOL: is warm to the touch and feels elastic and springy.

SILK: feels warm, smooth and elastic.

RAYON: feels cool, smooth, inelastic and generally lacks the feel of silk.

BURN TEST:

The simplest and easiest test leading to the identification of fabrics has been selected because it requires no equipment other than a few matches. The "burning" test for natural fibers cannot guarantee complete and accurate results, but enables some synthetic fabrics to be eliminated when silk is wanted. Before actually burning the small sample of fabric to be tested, move it slowly toward a small flame (a match or a candle) and observe the burning rate and possible odors emanating from the burning sample. Rayon and acetate burn so differently that you will have no difficulty distinguishing them from other fabrics.

COTTON: Cotton yarn blazes quickly. The ash is light and feathery and has an odor similar to that of burning paper. Mercerized cotton produces a black ash.

LINEN: Linen, when burned, produces an ash similar to cotton ash, light and feathery with a similar odor of burnt paper. It burns somewhat more slowly than cotton, but this is not a reliable factor. (See below: BREAKING TEST)

WOOL: Wool ignites slowly, and shows a characteristic small slow flickering flame that sizzles and curls, and it stops burning when the flame is withdrawn.

The ash is dark and crisp, falling into an irregular shape that can be crushed easily. It has an odor like that of burning hair or burning feathers.

SILK: Pure silk burns slowly and ceases burning when the flame is withdrawn. The ash of silk forms round, crisp, shiny black beads that crush easily. Since many silks are weighted or "filled," some of these burn without showing a visible flame. The burned part becomes incandescent, chars and smolders away, leaving a fragile skeleton of the original fabric.

RAYON: Rayon fabrics ignite and burn quickly and with a bright yellow flame. The ash disintegrates.

ACETATE: Acetate blazes as it burns; the edges of the fabric pucker and curl as the material fuses and melts into a hard mass.

BREAK TEST:

This is another simple method of identifying a fabric, more interesting than practical, but fun to try. First unravel a thread about 12in (30.5cm) long. Untwist the thread gently to restore it to its natural shape. Also pull apart gently when testing, so as not to interfere with the characteristic pattern of the fiber.

COTTON: Cotton yarns which are made from short staple fiber will show broken ends that are short, even and fuzzy, brush-like. You will note a curl at the ends, caused by the natural twisting of the fiber. Cotton fiber snaps when pulled apart.

LINEN: If linen thread resists breaking, untwist a little at a time until it snaps. The ends show long, straight, lustrous fibers that are pointed and uneven at the tip, and there is no curl.

WOOL: Wool thread has a fuzzy surface, stretches easily when the breaking test is applied, and the fiber ends are wavy and spiral.

SILK: Silk yarn stretches easily when pulled and breaks apart with a snap. The broken ends appear fine and lustrous and tend to "float" in the air.

RAYON: If tension is applied to a rayon thread, it appears strong and inelastic. If moistened with the tongue, a slight pull will then break the thread easily.

COTTON-LINEN: To distinguish between these two fabrics the following tests may be applied:

1. SQUEEZE: Pull a thread through tightly compressed fingertips. Linen thread will emerge stiff and straight, cotton will be limp and drooping.

2. TEAR THE FABRIC: Linen fabrics do not tear readily, whereas cotton tears easily with a characteristic shrill sound.

3. MOISTURE TEST: A common practice, although not very reliable particularly if you are comparing sheer cottons, is to place a drop of saliva on the under surface of the fabric. Linen is believed to absorb the moisture quickly, more slowly for cotton.

The above techniques will be more useful to you if you experiment with some fabrics already known to you as being certain kinds. These will enable you to recognize the characteristics described and to make comparisons between known fabrics and those you are testing. You will be more secure about identifying fabrics of which the fiber content is unknown.

SECTION TWENTY-SIX
A Last Word On The Subject Of Doll Costuming

We have come full circle from our introduction in which we suggested that dolls might be costumed in delightful replicas of old costumes. Again we reiterate that these are only substitutes for the "real thing" but many hours of enjoyable planning and sewing will result in the reward of seeing your doll look her best. Many people have suggested in recent books and articles about costuming that if old clothing must be replaced for aesthetic reasons, then plan to keep the old garments for reference.

Old garments do, indeed, provide a handy reference to the period from which your doll came, and might be used as models for styling other dolls in authentic fashion. (Note that this theory applies to collectors of "collectible" dolls as well, and for precisely the same reasons.) Old dresses may be examined for methods of construction typical of a certain period, trims may be significant and unusual, and fabrics might lead you to search for old garments or new fabrics with which to duplicate a dress. In any case, much learning may be achieved by observing what is at hand.

Our efforts here have been devoted to facilitating this process; our observations, our many years of trial and error, of working with every conceivable kind of antique doll, are here shared with all of you who likewise share our interest in doll costuming.

Insofar as is possible, we have used sound and established sources upon which to base all of the construction details and all of the fashions shown in this book, relying upon these references to substantiate our observations. If we have managed to put across to new collectors, who will be the doll costumers of the future, some of the important details and results of our experience, the efforts put into this book will be well justified. If at the same time we have added a little to the vast knowledge of costuming already enjoyed by old-timers like ourselves, that is indeed another bonus to be anticipated. So we leave it all now . . . to all of you. Good luck!

ADDENDUM
ABOUT DELINEATORS and PATTERNS

Most of us take our fine patterns with all of their intricate instructions and perfect sizing for granted. But can you imagine being without them?

Because of our interest in patterns and their development we have amassed a few facts about the early fashion books, and thought you might enjoy them also.

According to a *Metropolitan Monthly* of February 1874, the Butterick Company started printing patterns in 1865, issuing a *Metropolitan Monthly* as a means of illustrating and advertising their patterns. In 1872 they started publishing their *Delineator* to provide more scope in a larger publication for their patterns, with many more pictures in all categories and sizes including patterns for dolls. *The Delineator* achieved immediate popularity at a cost of 15¢ per issue or a year's subscription offered at $1.50 that included a choice of bonus patterns to a value of $1.00. Prices of individual patterns ranged from 20¢ to 40¢ with a deluxe version sometimes reaching $1.50.

How popular is "popular?" By 1883 circulation was 155,000 copies per month, and ten years later in 1893 it had reached the staggering number of 500,000. Circulation was worldwide, including 85 countries in such exotic and out-of-the-way places as Ceylon, Chile, Hong Kong, Congo, Curacao, Fiji Islands, Siam, Sierra Leone, Tasmania, Zanzibar, and Orange Free State. Of course the United States and Canada no doubt subscribed to a large percentage of the total output, but can we just imagine a lady of fashion strolling about in the bush country of Africa wearing her, oh, so fashionable full-skirted, many petticoated costume? It was, in fact, an established practice of the British (the ubiquitous British who were indeed everywhere in their colonial world during this period) to dress for dinner every night even when dining alone, alone in the jungle!

Subscription prices were reasonable enough, at $1.00 per year in the United States and Canada, and $1.60 yearly elsewhere. We do not know what inflation was doing or not doing to the economy in those days, but In 1905 Butterick points out that their *Delineator* magazine was still selling at 15¢ per copy, a price unchanged from 1872.

According to accounts of this era Butterick achieved phenomenal success with their patterns because of appropriate sizing which more nearly conformed to the female form than that of other pattern makers of the time. Butterick, it was said, had developed a "secret" system of establishing proportions, departing from the practice of other companies who had the idea that these things (sizing for patterns) must be done according to "correct" laws of proportions as found in antique statues . . . Venus de Milo? One can imagine a very correct Mr. Butterick going home with an appeal to his wife to measure herself, the upstairs maid and the plump cook, all of whom in turn probably checked on their friends to find out what ladies actually measured under their voluminous dresses. Whatever the system, they were apparently very successful. According to the same article, Butterick was producing about 15,000 patterns per day, and sending them out to all of the places mentioned earlier.

By 1897 Butterick was not only showing patterns in their *Delineator* magazines, but offered a wide variety of booklets on every conceivable subject of interest to women from sewing to child care, housekeeping and homemaking, crafts deportment, etc.

They introduced the DELTOR in 1929, an involved and explicit set of instructions for sewing, fitting, cutting, etc. For many of you reading this article you will remember the days of the more modern *Delineator* patterns, which were finally discontinued in 1937, although Butterick patterns are still with us.

SELECTED BIBLIOGRAPHY

Arnold, J. *Patterns of Fashion.* Wace & Co. Ltd. London 1966.

Bailey, Albina. *Dressing Dolls in 19th Century Fashions.* Athena Publishing Co. Missouri 1975.

Bradfield, N. *Historical Costumes of England 1066-1968.* Barnes & Noble Inc. New York, N. Y. 1972.

Brandon, Ruth. *A Capitalist Romance . . Singer and the Sewing Machine.* J. B. Lipincott Company, New York 1977.

Coleman, Dorothy, Elizabeth A. and Evelyn J. *The Collectors Book of Dolls Clothes.*

Cunningham, C. Willett and Phyllis. *Handbook of English Costume in the 19th Century.* Faber & Faber, London 1970 (Third Edition.)

———— *Complete Family Sewing Book.* Playmore 1979.

Dyer, Elizabeth. *Textile Fabrics.* The Riverside Press 1923.

———— *Instant Sewing.* Graphic Enterprises Inc. Grosset & Dunlop, New York 1968.

Lynch, Mary & Dorothy Sara. *Sewing Made Easy.* Garden City Books, Garden City, N. Y. 1952.

Potter, D. M. and Corbman, Bernard. *Textiles: Fiber to Fabric.* McGraw-Hill Book Company 1967.

———— *Simplicity Diary and Calendar 1980.*

INDEX